D1601361

The Modern Kleinian Approach to Psychoanalytic Technique

The Modern Kleinian Approach to Psychoanalytic Technique

Clinical Illustrations

ROBERT WASKA, MFT, PhD

JASON ARONSON
Lanham • Boulder • New York • Toronto • Plymouth, UK

Published by Jason Aronson
An imprint of Rowman & Littlefield Publishers, Inc.
A wholly owned subsidary of The Rowman & Littlefield Publishing Group, Inc.
4501 Forbes Boulevard, Suite 200, Lanham, Maryland 20706
http://www.rowmanlittlefield.com

Estover Road, Plymouth PL6 7PY, United Kingdom

British Library Cataloguing in Publication Information Available

Library of Congress Cataloging-in-Publication Data

Waska, Robert T.
  The modern Kleinian approach to psychoanalytic technique : clinical illustrations /
Robert Waska.
     p. ; cm.
  Includes bibliographical references and index.
  ISBN 978-0-7657-0784-0 (cloth : alk. paper) — ISBN 978-0-7657-0786-4 (electronic)
  1. Klein, Melanie. 2. Psychoanalysis. I. Title.
  [DNLM: 1. Klein, Melanie. 2. Psychoanalytic Therapy—methods. 3. Psychoanalytic
Theory. WM 460.6 W319m 2010]
  RC504.W295 2010
  616.89'17—dc22

                                                                2010006373

⊗™ The paper used in this publication meets the minimum requirements of American
National Standard for Information Sciences—Permanence of Paper for Printed Library
Materials, ANSI/NISO Z39.48-1992.

Printed in the United States of America

Contents

Preface

Melanie Klein's pioneering work with children and adults expanded Freud's clinical work and is now the leading worldwide influence in current psychoanalytic practice. The key Kleinian concepts include the total transference, projective identification, the importance of countertransference, psychic retreats, the container/contained function, enactment, splitting, the paranoid and depressive positions, unconscious phantasy, and the value of interpreting both anxiety and defense. The components of the Kleinian approach have become so commonplace in the literature and adopted by so many other schools of practice that it is easy to forget that Object Relations theory and technique was Melanie Klein's discovery.

In broadening Klein's work to match today's clinical climate, I have developed (Waska 2005, 2006, 2007) the use of Kleinian technique in all aspects of clinical practice, with all patients, in all settings. I call this approach Analytic Contact. By analytic contact, I mean that the therapist/analyst should always attempt to engage the patient in an exploration of their unconscious phantasies, transference patterns, defenses, and internal experience of the world. Regardless of frequency, use of couch, length of treatment, or style of termination, the goal of psychoanalytic treatment is always the same: the understanding of unconscious phantasy, the resolution of intra-psychic conflict, and the integration of self/object relations, both internally and externally. The psychoanalyst uses interpretation as a principal tool, with transference, countertransference, and projective identification being the three clinical guideposts of those interpretive efforts. Viewed from the Kleinian perspective, most patients utilize projective identification as a psychic cornerstone for defense, communication, attachment, learning, loving, and aggression. As such, projective identification constantly shapes and colors both the transference and countertransference.

By attending to the interpersonal, transactional, and intra-psychic levels of transference and phantasy with consistent here-and-now and in-the-moment interpretation, the Kleinian method can be therapeutically successful with neurotic, borderline, narcissistic, or psychotic patients, whether being seen as individuals, couples, or families and at varied frequencies and duration.

The Kleinian method of Analytic Contact strives to illuminate the patient's unconscious object relational world, gradually providing the patient a way to understand, express, translate, and master their previously unbearable thoughts and feelings. We make analytic contact with their deepest experiences so they can make personal and lasting contact with their full potential.

Successful analytic contact involves not only psychic change, but a corresponding sense of loss and mourning. So, every moment analytic contact is both an experience of hope and transformation as well as dread and despair as the patient struggles with change and a new way of being with himself and others. Successful analytic work always results in a cycle of fearful risk taking, hasty retreats, retaliatory attacks, anxious detours, and attempts to shift the treatment into something less than analytic, something less painful. The analyst interprets these reactions to the precarious journey of growth as a way of steering the treatment back to something more analytic, something that contains more meaningful contact with self and other. The support that we give our patients includes the inherent vow that we will help them survive this painful contact and walk with them into the unknown.

In working from a Kleinian perspective, the modern psychoanalyst utilizes three components in their daily technique. The concept of the total transference (Klein 1952; Joseph 1985), the phenomenon of projective identification, and the clinical importance of understanding the countertransference as well as the resulting enactments created by the interpersonal pressure of various projections. These are the primary tools used in clinical practice to help the patient come closer in touch with their core phantasies and work through their fundamental anxieties.

However, the transference profile of our typical patient, especially the more disturbed and uncontained individuals we often see in private practice settings, is one that is fleeting, confusing, and difficult to clinically summarize. In fact, it is frequently hard to locate the transference or the core phantasy and anxiety a patient is living with.

Chapter 1 explores how this lack of analytic footing can occur with transference states that are bold, loud, and sharp or with seemingly absent transference states that are quiet, soft, and obscure. When we do begin to have a momentary understanding of our patient's dynamics and the various projections that make up these murky transferences, we are often caught off guard by it seeming to change entirely or to disappear altogether. Sometimes, the countertransference is painful as we feel adrift for long periods of time without any real sense of what is happening in the transference and therefore no immediate method of interpreting it. Two cases are presented in this chapter. One case represents the clinical movements of a loud and perplexing transference state, and the other case illustrates moments within a soft and unformed transference state. Ways of locating the essence of meaning within these states and how to tolerate long periods of uncertainty are discussed.

Chapter 2 continues to examine the cases encountered in psychoanalytic practice in which the transference is either loud, sharp, and obvious or quiet, soft, and difficult to locate. In both circumstances, the loud or soft transference states can be complex, confusing, and difficult to interpret with any ongoing clarity. The reasons for this appear to be a variety of defensive dynamics based around projective identification mechanisms that create multiple psychological conflict zones which are fast moving and quickly interchangeable.

More case material is used to show the importance of moment-to-moment transference and countertransference monitoring followed by here-and-now interpretations that may not be accurately summarizing the complete arc of the transference but instead capture the current and immediate anxiety of the patient's phantasy world at that particular clinical juncture.

Chapter 3 brings the reader's attention to those patients who are trapped within phantasies concerning the conflicts and consequences of giving and receiving. These cases initially appear to be either depressive in nature or more persecutory and within the borderline/narcissistic realm of functioning. However, the case material in chapter 3 will illustrate how in the transference a mixed psychological dilemma of both paranoid (Klein 1946) and depressive

(Klein 1935, 1940) conflicts emerge, centered around warped visions of what is being given and what is being taken. For these patients, the object is in desperate need of healing and attention but can also become attacking and depriving. The object can at once be the fountain of much needed nurturing and love as well as the sudden source of betrayal and attack. So, when working closely with the transference, countertransference, and the constant impact of projective identification mechanisms, the analyst will uncover these tangled profiles of both lower- and higher-functioning psychological states and find the patient to be struggling with a truly confusing and unbalancing internal storm. Desire, need, control, loss, and dread are only some of the constant specters in these types of treatments. Careful maintenance of analytic contact can allow for the gradual working through of the patient's intense anxiety, grief, envy, and need for control. This working through can hopefully usher in a more balanced experience of giving and receiving.

Chapter 4 continues the theme of exploring complicated varieties of pathology in the realm of giving, pleasing, and controlling the object. Using case material, this chapter examines patients who are emotionally confined within a very primitive experience of depressive conflict between self and object. The desire to please the object is a mix of wanting to favor approval and love from the hoped-for good object, but this need to please also serves to appease the potentially angry object and avoid any conflict that could trigger abandonment, rejection, or persecution.

These pre-depressive, immature depressive, or prematurely depressive patients can also exhibit angry demand, rejection, and cold self-absorption as an identification with the bad object, or they can exhibit an overly exaggerated sense of loyalty and generosity as an identification with the hoped-for, idealized good object.

Splitting and projective identification are often the vehicles for chronic and pathological cycles of relating as well as ways of establishing and maintaining rigid and destructive images of self and object. Dedicated, moment-to-moment work within the total transference, the complete countertransference, all projective dynamics, and the interpretive process are necessary to establish and maintain sufficient analytic contact to begin working through some of these complicated and difficult clinical situations.

Chapter 5 begins a series of reflections on the technical complexities of working analytically with patients who are clinically vexing, emotionally stormy, and primitively organized. These are borderline and narcissistic patients who exhibit severe internal clashes between love and hate, life and death, need and distance, and stances of retreat and attack. Analytic contact is the constant goal with failure along the way to be expected. However, with clinical perseverance, these moments of defeat or collapse do not always have to be complete or permanent. Indeed, there can be remarkable and important progress, growth, and change achieved with these individuals when both parties are willing to stick it out and create a break in the psychological storm.

Using two extensive case reports in chapter 5, the author examines the difficulty some patients have with separation, individuation, and autonomy. For these patients, operating within a fragile and immature level of depressive functioning, difference and independent thought or identity are considered taboo and dangerous to both self and object. Therefore, in these clinical situations, the transference and countertransference become infused with great conflict regarding mutuality, need, and self-expression. Patients struggling with these types of phantasies over-rely on projective identification which can then easily bring about various levels of acting out by both patient and analyst. In both cases presented, the analyst's enactment, triggered by projective identification dynamics, produced a tremendous reaction in the patient, based on the patient's volatile and primitive depressive phantasies regarding the meaning of allowing the object to be less than ideal, less than controlled and predictable, and more than simply a mirror image of the self.

In chapter 6, the author uses two case examples to continue examining the difficult reality of private practice work for the contemporary psychoanalyst. Rather than the idealized portrait of multiple visits on the couch with a neurotic patient who stays for years until fully working through various issues, the actual researched reality of clinical work is not as neat and tidy. It is not unusual to meet with a fairly disturbed individual who only attends once a week, acts out quite a bit, and ultimately terminates not long after beginning the treatment. Most cases examined in the literature are those that fit the more traditional or more idealized picture of what psychoanalysis is, which creates a false portrayal of how psychoanalysts really serve those who are in need. We have many cases we succeed with and many that we fail at. And, the ones that seem to be a failure by idealized unrealistic standards may really be a successful containment or safety net provided in a moment of great crisis even if not an overall psychological transformation. This chapter suggests this momentary containment or brief analytic contact to still be psychoanalytic in nature. Only by exploring all the different aspects of how we practice and with whom we practice can we come to understand the value of our theories and whether we need to strengthen them, change them, or confidently rely on them.

The two case reports in chapter 6 show the use of the psychoanalytic method with difficult and disturbed patients who cannot tolerate the exploration of their emotional conflicts for very long before they need to flee. Both these patients struggled with intense paranoid and depressive phantasies which made the working-through process stormy and ultimately impossible. Even though these types of patients often abort treatment after only a handful of sessions or sometimes after a rocky few months, the Kleinian approach of Analytic Contact is presented as a helpful method that can sometimes provide valuable, even if temporary, aid to the unbearable psychic pain that makes up this type of patient's internal experiences.

Chapter 7 continues this focus on hard-to-reach patients by examining the clinical struggles of working with narcissistic patients. The Kleinian approach to understanding narcissism is discussed with emphasis on Herbert Rosenfeld's contributions. An extensive case study of a libidinal narcissist is presented, followed by a contrasting case of a more destructive narcissistic character.

The use of pathological forms of splitting and projective identification is highlighted as well as the common narcissistic phantasies that emerge over conflicts with difference, dependence, and control. Finally, the combination of interpretation and confrontation is explored as a helpful technique with the more libidinal narcissist, who typically is suffering within a closed system of both depressive and paranoid phantasies.

Acknowledgments

This book is the result of the interaction between my patients and the complex, intriguing clinical situations that I have been invited into. I thank all my patients for allowing me into their unique and complicated unconscious mindscape and for showing me a glimpse of how rich, creative, and intricate the human condition can be. All case material has been altered, changed, or disguised to maintain confidentiality.

I am always grateful to my wife, Elizabeth, who provides balance, joy, and vision to my work and to my life. As an emerging artist, she has created the image for the cover of this book.

Finally, I wish to thank Jason Aronson for their help in bringing this project to fruition.

I

TWO MODES OF PHANTASY AND TRANSFERENCE

1

Soft and Quiet, Hard and Loud

Two Types of Complex Transference States

As we try to uncover and follow the tracks of our patient's paranoid (Klein 1946) and depressive (Klein 1935, 1940) struggles, we can often feel clueless and misinformed. While we are trying to find the tail of the transference or while we grapple with what the meaning might be of the patient's overt transference dynamics, we can experience our own paranoid and depressive uncertainty. Some patients are initially unable to express their anxieties in words so they express themselves in other ways, such as acting out or turning towards an intense focus on various external situations.

Many of our patients are dealing with the inability to be alone. They are not able to feel whole, soothed, or important by themselves. The sense of solitude or loneliness that comes with realizing one is a unique, separate individual is intolerable to many patients and creates a sense of fragmentation, abandonment, and persecution. While acceptance and integration of this internal solitude is part of healthy growth and internal integrity, many of our patients find it unbearable and act out these fears in the transference (Quinodoz 1996).

During these stressful moments, the patient will often project this unbearable loneliness or depression into the analyst. In this state, the analyst may feel lost and depressed at not being able to find the transference, understand it, or interpret with precision. Quinodoz (1993) points out how the "tamed" sense of solitude is a hallmark of the mature depressive position. Unfortunately, I think most of our more difficult patients are struggling with a "wild and un-tamed" experience of loneliness, desperation, and alienation that pushes them to hide, run, and attack instead of trying to face, accept, and tame. So, while helping the patient to name it, claim it, and tame it is our ultimate therapeutic goal, I believe most of our patients are busy disclaiming their internal conflicts and running from the wild beast they feel is within them. This sort of internal state can create intense transference conditions that are either very difficult to trace and understand or overwhelming and confusing.

Due to the projective identification cycle usually involved in this situation, the analyst may feel lost for minutes, days, or even weeks, wondering where the transference is, what it is, and what to do about it. This countertransference situation can create a paranoid persecution, a lonely lost depressive state, or a difficult but manageable and healthy depressive loneliness and solitude.

Case material is used to illustrate this state of being lost or adrift with the patient for periods of time and the troubling countertransference that can ensue. However, if the countertransference is utilized as a compass in this temporary blindness and if the analyst's tracking of the core unconscious phantasy state is used as a map to the possible projective identification dynamics that may be obscuring the analyst's vision, then clinical clarity can be restored.

CASE #1

With some patients, the transference is so bold and intense that the analyst can easily observe there to be a transference occurring of some sort. This is initially helpful because even though we know there to be a transference process occurring in every treatment regardless if we can locate it or not, it is certainly reassuring when we see signs of this phenomenon right in front of us. But, in many cases, it still remains a formidable task to place this dynamic in context to the patient's core phantasies or central anxieties. What we see being acted out is not necessarily the most important aspect of the patient's struggles or the most defended. However, it certainly gives us a starting point.

So, in the countertransference, it often feels reassuring to see some kind of intense or obvious transference process. Then, I feel I have something to work with or investigate, rather than feel lost, failing, or alone. However, when the transference acting out is intense, it can be confusing or difficult in other ways.

Initially, Sandra had called me to "discuss what she was going to do with her life and to deal with some feelings she didn't understand too well." We set up a tentative appointment, but I told her I would need to call her back within a few days to confirm it as there was a potential problem which would mean we would need to meet a few days later.

Sandra had told me during that first phone call that she was seventy years old. Two days later, Sandra called me several times. She said, "I wanted to find out if you still have the time to see me. I understand you may not want to see someone my age, as I may seem too old and probably just full of use-less complaints. I do hope you will give me a chance to talk with you. Then, I think you will understand I am living a full life and have a great capac-ity for conversation and creativity." Sandra seemed to worry I was already discounting her as too old and not possibly interesting enough to hold my attention.

Sandra was seventy years old but dressed like she was a hip thirty- or forty-year-old. She wore modern clothing and had her hair done with a bold dye. She looked like she had an enhancement procedure to her lips, making them overly plump and pouty. In the countertransference, I felt she was a bit "weird," needy, and pushy. During the first few sessions, Sandra spoke with me in ways that communicated strong views of herself and her objects. She related to me in ways that showed she needed to control the object and was convinced the object would try and control her.

Right off the bat, Sandra informed me that "I know I am abrasive. Many people have told me that and that is just the way it is. Most people don't like me." I said, "You are worried if I will want to be with you or not? You are worried if you will turn me away too?" She replied, "I don't really care. I am paying you to listen to me. I presume you could fire me, but I could fire you too." Here, I was introduced to the abrasive and arrogant manner that she would be with me in the following months.

Even though there were these strong, blatant transference movements, I was not immediately sure of what the principle phantasies and anxieties were. I felt we would have to take the ride together for awhile before I knew. Here, I was experiencing a healthy depressive tension but on occasion also felt the sharp pang of a more paranoid fear of "maybe she will fire me without warn-ing." For the most part, I had a tentative impression that Sandra was dealing with grandiose, narcissistic views of herself that were extremely fragile and prone to collapse into worthlessness and desolation which were paired with envy and contempt for her objects.

During a session in the first month of treatment, Sandra told me she was going to cancel her next appointment and several weeks afterwards in order to recover from a face-lift procedure. I asked her why she wanted this, and she told me she "wanted to feel and look refreshed." I asked if she felt old, and she stared at me and laughed. She said, "I never feel old! I just wanted to get rid of a few of these wrinkles." Here, I was once again not so sure what exactly was happening in the transference. I felt some contempt for her as she seemed so self-absorbed to be telling me to cancel our visits for several weeks to get a face-lift. But, I also thought she seemed desperate to add to her narcissistic armor and thicken her walls to ward off some type of terrible anxiety.

So, I simply said I thought it was unfortunate—we had just started meeting, and now we would have to stop so soon. She agreed but said nothing else until the next session when she told me she had cancelled the procedure since she "thought it might be painful and a bit dangerous." Here, I sensed she had responded to my query about her stopping the treatment and my pondering her need for the procedure and then had decided to change course.

After I asked her to tell me about herself, Sandra began telling me about her past. She told me that she was brought up in a very poor family on a farm in a small rural town. Her father was an angry and sometimes violent alcoholic. Sandra's mother did her best to take care of the five children but was usually tired, depressed, and resolved about her fate. At age sixteen, Sandra left home for New York, where she hoped to escape the ravages of her chaotic home life. I said, "You were trying to be independent and save yourself, but that must have been very difficult since you were at an age where you still needed to depend on them and have them take care of you." Sandra said, "You have to deal with what is in front of you. I had no choice. I was excited to go to the big city, to see Broadway and Times Square!"

She said all this in an almost defiant manner that felt like she was establishing herself as strong and unaffected by others. This "have to deal with what is in front of you" defense seemed to have some cracks as Sandra called me the next day to check and see if she had the right time for the next appointment. On her message, she told me that talking about the past has made her feel "surprisingly" quite down and that she was looking forward to talking next time. So, this was evidence of a transference in which she showed off as an independent woman who was above it all and able to take care of business. Indeed, she mentioned several times how she put herself through college and ended up a successful businesswoman respected by all her male peers. At the same time, telling me about her past seemed to open old wounds and make her temporarily rely on me for either comfort, reassurance, or simply a quick fix at the pit stop before she got back in the race.

An example of this more aggressive way of dealing with or rather controlling her vulnerability came out over her payments. During one session, Sandra asked me to sign a handwritten paper that showed the dates we met and the amount of money she had paid me. I told her I would be happy to give her a receipt at the end of every month when I do my bookwork, but I wondered why she needed this now. She told me she wanted to "protect herself and it was just good common business sense." "As a businessman, you should certainly realize that!" she said. I said it seemed she was worried about something, maybe being taken advantage of by me in some way. Sandra immediately replied, "I have been taken advantage of before and I quickly learned how to prevent that. Are you going to sign it?" I said, "I wonder if you mean you have been taken advantage of emotionally as well as financially. You seem to want to make sure you are protected against both." She told me, "I have been taken advantage of emotionally before. But, right now, I am asking you if you are going to sign it or not." I said, "It sounds like an or-else question." She said, "Well, if you won't sign it, I don't know if I can continue. I want to make sure I am covered."

So, we continued to discuss this, and I tried to make sense of this for myself and with Sandra. But, besides the obvious sense of control, persecution, and mistrust, I was left unsure of what may lay behind these anxieties. Here, I was wondering if she was trying to head off something that had already happened, a fear of the future that was really about the past (Winnicott 1974). In other words, there was a phantasy of betrayal and need of protection already taking place in the transference that was a repeat of something in the past, but she was concretely seeing it as something that could happen in the future.

I thought I had settled the concrete aspect of this receipt problem by trying to contain it with exploration, interpretation, and limit setting. I thought we had analyzed the emotional aspect a bit but overall had only touched the tip of what was an unclear but noticeable mistrust and struggle for dominance or control. So, when Sandra arrived for the next session and I confirmed a date for the following week and she told me "it didn't matter because this would be our last time," I was not surprised. I had a feeling from the first time I met her that our attachment was tenuous, fragile, and prone to instant collapse without warning or reason. Here, I think I was also a victim to the fear of breakdown (Winnicott 1974) when in fact it was a breakdown that had already occurred and was still occurring as we went forward. I asked her why, and she told me that since I "refused to sign the receipts, she could not trust me and could not continue. She would not leave herself so vulnerable and if I could not understand her position it was fine and my right, but she would not continue." It was a standoff, and I realized she meant it. So, I told her I could see that she was serious and would not talk about the meaning of it without me doing it. So, I said, "If it means we would part unless I sign it, I will sign it."

But, then I said I felt this was indicative of how much she struggled with getting close to me and others. I said that on one hand she wanted to trust and be a part of things, but she was so convinced she would be hurt that she had to put up walls to feel safer and have a say. I suggested that this "either sign it or else" standoff could be part of how she sees the world and why others might see her as "abrasive." Sandra agreed and said she could see my point but the signing of the receipt "was more about the money." She said she "was only being careful to not end up in a situation where if someone questioned whether she had paid or not, she wanted to have proof." I said she seemed to think I would turn around and accuse her of not paying and then demand more money. Sandra clarified it and told me, "Not exactly. It is more the idea that if something happened to you, your trustees could look at your records and if you hadn't recorded my payments, they would come after me. You could fall dead of a heart attack, or your office might burn to the ground with all the records. So, I just want a personal record and proof of my payment. That only seems right."

Here I was once again in a state of countertransference uncertainty. I felt there were certainly clear and intense transference dynamics at work regarding trust, persecution, loss, and so forth. There was a phantasy of me being killed off and her facing the persecutory fallout of that murder. But, I also felt there were other dynamics in the air which I did not understand yet. So, while I could certainly see how she was holding us for ransom by demanding I sign the receipts or she would leave for good, I did not anticipate the other piece of the puzzle that came at the end of the session. As she was leaving, Sandra told me, "I am glad you ended up signing the receipts. I would have hated to lose you." Here, she seemed both genuinely relieved at not losing me but also aloof, as if she was glad to not have to go through the trouble of contacting the maid service to request a replacement servant.

I was struck by how she split me and our relationship into two portions so quickly. I first felt she was insulting me, showing off her superior hand and how she could so easily dismiss or discard me. At the same time, I immediately had the sense she was relieved that she was not alone, that our tie had not been broken. She had not killed me off or lost me. Sandra was happy she had not destroyed our bond but had to put that tension and relief into me. Now, I felt I had another piece of the puzzle. I was still unsure of what exactly we were up against in the big picture, but the moment-to-moment analyst work was proceeding.

This crisscross type of transference relating continued. A short period of time after the receipt standoff, Sandra created another contrasting method of viewing me, relating to me, and controlling me. She came into a session and looked me over, sat down, and said, "You look very handsome in that blue shirt, very handsome. It really makes you pop. You have good taste. It shows off your face and makes you look quite distinguished." So, here I felt she was flirting with me in a way that put her in control but also was a gift of an affectionate gaze. However, the sense of her lauding this over me leaked through in her next comments which shifted the transference climate dramatically.

Sandra said, "That haircut makes you look gay. I don't think there is anything wrong with that but it does make you look very effeminate. I would think you would realize that and visit a barber who knows better." So, again, there was a clear set of transference projections in play but the underlying motive, internal desires, and anxieties that made up the phantasies were still unclear.

We often never know the whole-picture transference with such disturbed patients since they live in a fragmented jagged world and project only sections and chunks instead of whole object relational phantasy states. Therefore, we must work in the dark for most of the treatment in many of these cases, relying only on the clarity of the moment-to-moment total transference situation and the nature of the projective identification process in the current analytic setting, which then may change dramatically by the next session or even in the next ten minutes.

This ongoing uncertainty can cause several unhealthy reactions in the countertransference, leading to enactments unless properly monitored and managed. On one hand, the analyst may become anxious and try and pin down, control, and fix this vague and unknown transference state. The desire to know may take on pathological proportions, and the analyst may resort to more supportive counseling and "life coaching" in order to feel they have an understanding and a handle on the transference and phantasy states.

At the other extreme, the analyst may become complacent (Britton 1998) and therapeutically coast as a way to feel relief from this worry and uncertainty. As a result, these types of defensive treatment states will start to look like agreeable, easygoing social gatherings that don't focus on deep material but simply check off the appropriate areas of discussion and rely mostly on talking about current events in the patient's life with some empathic counseling along the way.

Another manner in which this complacency can emerge is when the analyst settles into only interpreting one level of transference (Roth 2001). The complacent interpretation of "and me too" where everything is simply interpreted as an unconscious reference to the analyst is one way this can occur. Even more detached can be the settling into a level of interpretation where only the patient's feelings about their actual external object of reference are explored. Cangnan (2004) notes how Kleinian analysts strive to help the patient learn about themselves and see knowledge of the self as indicative of integration, growth, and creativity. This knowledge and the search for it can be resisted by both patient and analyst. So, not only can the patient or analyst become complacent as a defense against change and identity, but either party can attack new knowledge and work aggressively to maintain the current psychic equilibrium (Joseph 1989), even if the status quo is stale, painful, or pathological.

Another aspect of the total transference situation that arose within the first few months of Sandra's analytic treatment was her view of how I treated her. When I began and ended on time, she felt I was being "tight and rigid, a real clock watcher." I interpreted that while I was just ending on time, she seemed to feel I was throwing her out. Sandra said, "Well, I guess it is just a business after all." So, she seemed to have decided I was only going to treat her as a business commodity at best and quickly get rid of her when her time was up. She would not allow for the vision of caring *and* ending on time. She told me I "was cold that way."

As with all patients, I asked Sandra to pay at the start of each session. Sandra reacted to this by telling me I "was awfully quick to ask for money. You seem to really focus on the payment, like that is all you care about." Here, I felt she was aggressively and powerfully assigning me a certain bad status in her mind without any room for change or for clarification. I was now stamped "a clock watcher and focused on money" and that was it. I felt unable to escape that decision. With that finality in mind from my countertransference, I said, "You seemed to have decided I am not a very good guy in all these ways without giving me much of a chance and without any room to sort out what I really might be like. You have labeled me, and that is that." Sandra said, "I call it like I see it."

At this point, the analytic situation with Sandra was intense and precarious. She saw me as an object she hoped to depend on but was quick to devalue and reject. Sandra's desire for a union with a helper and healer is quickly twisted by her narcissistic demand and fragile ego into demands for loyalty and allegiance or else. When she told me she is abrasive and no one likes her, I think this is the reason. She creates a relationship in which she actively makes you into someone who doesn't like her or that she is convinced doesn't want her so then she will have to leave first. At the same time, in a very convoluted and prickly manner, Sandra does seem to want to establish contact and explore her anxieties.

Sandra spent a couple of weeks telling me about her first of two marriages. In recollecting this first ten-year marriage, Sandra related a "great deal of disappointment, and looking back I feel I wasted so many years of my life." I told her I thought she wanted to tell me her story so that she could begin sorting it out and perhaps grieve for those wasted years and understand how she had gotten into what she so regretted. This interpretation was my response to her spontaneously bringing it up in a manner that seemed calculated, matter of fact, but emotionally important to her in an effort to perhaps better understand herself but definitely rid herself of strong feelings of regret and grief.

In telling me about the marriage, I noticed the same type of two-tiered feelings that colored the transference. Sandra both idealized herself while also feeling angry with herself for having failed in her current life at finding a way to feel important and occupied. She was also angry at others for trying to control her and treat her poorly instead of praising her and recognizing her as a good person deserving attention.

So, in her story, Sandra married a well-known lawyer who was the son of a famous and rich industrialist. Her husband's mother called all the shots and told them where to live, what clothes to wear, what parties to go to, and what country clubs to belong to. As I heard all the details, I noticed Sandra veered back and forth between seeming to show off and impress me with tales of money and high society, name dropping as she went, and then adding stories of how disrespected, mistreated, and depressed she was through those years. In other words, the total transference seemed to again be a combination of her wanting my help and compassion while making sure to put me in my place and let me know she was important and in charge.

Using Kleinian methods of understanding Sandra's anxieties, I came to think of her as living in a world of both paranoid and depressive conflicts. She seemed to be sure I could take advantage of her and she had plenty of stories of feeling attacked by others. She also seemed to use a manic strategy to prop herself up higher than others and quickly remind me of my lower status. She would feel sorry for me and others but in a sarcastic and devaluing sort of way. Finally, I felt irritated and turned off by her arrogant ways but then felt sorry for her and wanted to help her find a better way of experiencing herself and her objects. Here, it seemed the reparative aspects of the depressive position were projected into me and I was left to forgive and repair, even though she had initiated the battle or injury.

Bianchedi et al. (1988) notes how Klein extended Freud's ideas about separation anxiety when she explored the ego's recognition of dependence on objects and the danger of loss entailed. This concern brings on guilt and then the striving to repair and to find forgiveness. I think that this can be part of the projective identification process in which the intolerable or humiliating aspects of the depressive experience are put into the analyst to bear.

During the twelve weeks I met with Sandra, she demonstrated marked shifts of mood and dramatic turnabouts with her vision of self and object, all consistent with the more severe aspects of borderline and narcissistic functioning within the paranoid-schizoid spectrum. One week she was simply bored with life and the stale and silly ways of "all those around her," including me in the transference. Another week, she was "lost and lonely, deep in a place of utter desolation," in which she did not get out of bed for most of every day and spoke to no one. In a manic triumph over others who seemed to have love and importance, the next week she told me she was "cured" and "enjoyed laying in bed all day and doing as she pleased, unencumbered by the needs of others and the day-to-day stupidity of life." Another week, she claimed to have suddenly made friends, been approached by numerous men, and was ready to travel and go back to college.

This idea of being pursued by several men contained a kernel of her yearning for special attention and love but also her conviction of ultimately being rejected, mistreated, or used. First, she said she had no need for men, she "was done with them, they are of no use to me." I interpreted her reluctance to depend on me and see me as someone she could seek help from or get close to since she put me down and rendered me valueless. She told me, "The jury is still out on you, but you have yet to prove your worth."

At one point, she told me how she had attended a class at a local senior center and all the wives "went out of their way to protect their husbands from me, as if I was going to kidnap them." A week later, Sandra told me she received phone calls from several of the men asking her out when their wives were out of town. Sandra said she was "entertained, but put out that they just wanted to use her to fill their time while they waited for their wives to return."

Shortly after, she told me she was "profoundly touched that the teacher of the class, a man thirty years younger, was expressing interest in her." For a few days, Sandra was moved to the point of tears, telling me while weeping, "I had pretty much given up on the hope of anyone ever wanting me or loving me. I think he really likes me, and I have not felt touched by someone's honest interest in a very long time." A few days later, she was angry and disappointed that he had started calling her several times a day and wanted to have sex with her when his wife was away.

Sandra also had stories of being pursued by "a dirty old man" who lived in her apartment complex. Sandra thought it was disgusting and didn't want anything to do with him. But, I interpreted that she told me the story in a way that seemed to show her need for me to realize she was still pretty, viable, and wanted by others instead of forgotten. She responded by saying it was just one old and sick individual who had nothing better to do.

In the transference, I was a consistently shifting figure, stretching from good to bad and back again, mirroring Sandra's internal view of self as either ideal and perfect or old and cast away. Some days I was "cute, intelligent, and genuine, obviously a professional and responsive therapist." Other days, I was simply out for her money, "just running a business with paying customers."

Often, she thought I didn't understand her and "asked odd questions that didn't go in the direction she would have thought would be pertinent or useful to making her feel better."

Throughout the treatment, Sandra dropped hints and told stories about how she made a habit of "working the system." She received disability payments for something she had essentially made up ten years ago, and through an oversight, the government was still sending her a small payment every month. She said, "It is their fault, why should I call attention to it?" The class she took where the teacher had made advances was a class she wasn't really eligible for, but after she told them she really needed it for her degree, a lie, they agreed to enroll her. She told me she had taken another class only open to disabled persons and therefore the class was offered for free as compared to anywhere else where she would have to pay. So, she lied her way into it and paid nothing. She told me of defiantly installing a hot tub on her apartment porch against her neighborhood homeowner's policy, and when they told her to get rid of it, she agreed right away only to put up a covering that made it look like she had taken it down.

Meanwhile, I was having a great deal of difficulty getting her insurance company to respond to my billing, so as she told me more and more examples of her crafty manipulation and narcissistic use of others, I began to worry I would never be paid. I brought this up and added that it seemed part of a double-edged sword she brought in with her. If I brought it up, she would feel I was only in it for the money. If I didn't bring it up, I was giving her power over me and ending up feeling used. So, either way, one of us was going to feel used or betrayed by the other. There seemed to not be any middle ground to explore this type of interpersonal tension without the tension escalating.

When I said all this, she said, "Well, when you put it that way, I can see what you mean. I don't want you to feel that way. I am flabbergasted you think I am that type of person, who would stiff you. But, in any case, be assured I will pay personally for this treatment if the insurance fails." Here, I did believe her but was taken by the dual personality I felt I was with, both honest and direct and dishonest and sneaky.

Another manner in which the transference played out was when Sandi brought in her insurance copayment each time. In the beginning, she would never give me the money at the beginning without my reminding her, even though I had requested this pattern from day one. So, I was put in the position of reminding her each time, and she then told me I was always thinking of money and more interested in getting paid than listening to what was on her mind and of immediate concern. I interpreted this power struggle she initiated.

A few weeks later, Sandra would take the bills out of her purse and throw them at me. She would say, "Catch!" and fling the bills at me. They would fall to the floor, and I felt she clearly was placing me in a demeaning, inferior place of having to pick up my scraps of cash off the floor. When I made this interpretation, Sandra quickly told me I was "quite mistaken. You just don't understand me. No one does. No one ever has. I am simply playing with you, poking fun and having fun. I am being friendly with you." I said, "That may be and that is very important. I want to know all about your feelings for me, both positive and negative. But, if you are being playful, it is in a sarcastic, aggressive sort of way that clouds the playfulness. When you tell me everyone finds you offensive and never wants to be your friend, could this be an example of how they misread your intentions?" Sandra said, "I suppose so, but I don't care what they think anymore. I don't need them. I am fine with myself."

This manic, narcissistic independence was a mask to enormous loneliness, self-loathing, and despair. However, Sandra was unable to allow herself to face these feelings for very long before retreating, and she would only let me into her chaotic, jarring internal world for brief moments before slamming the door shut, declaring herself omnipotent and the world useless. She abruptly, but not surprisingly, stopped attending after three months. She left me with a phone message that summed up these desperate defensive reactions to her objects and her inner conflicts. She said, "You have helped me as much as you were able to, doing your best to the capacity of your training. But, that was not enough. I have decided the matters we discussed were really of no use to me and did not address my needs. I hope you have a good life, and I thank you. You did the best you could. I will not be needing your services anymore. I am off to the bookstore for a self-help book. Adios."

Sandra's analytic treatment was only in the beginning stages when she terminated. As is, however, it was complicated and highly volatile, with her phantasies and defenses on the move constantly. As a result, it was difficult to keep up and make sense of the whole matter. Sandra was an example of a patient who presented a transference that was loud yet complicated and confusing. It was easy to see that a transference process was occurring by the direct references, both positive and negative, that Sandra made toward the analyst. These were what can be called "loud" transferences that are at the same time complex and confusing without any singular or immediately thematic pattern.

In situations like this one, the total transference situation can be so dense and shifting that the best technical path is to stay in the very immediate moment. This approach is very much in line with how Hargreaves and Varchevker (2004) outline Betty Joseph's work, which centers on examining everything the patient brings to the therapeutic relationship, respecting the patient's need to maintain their existing psychic equilibrium, despite consciously wanting to change. In addition, the investigation of projective identification and countertransference is considered therapeutically valuable along with the analyst remaining focused on the alive and immediate here-and-now clinical encounter and the avoidance of trying to control everything or know all about the patient right away. Indeed, we must endure not having control and not knowing everything while also believing we can acquire enough valuable insight to pass on to the patient by remaining religiously present in the close, current clinical situation

CASE #2

In this second case report, the treatment involved a "soft" transference profile in which it was difficult to locate, understand, or interpret any transference movement at all for extended periods of time. For long periods, the analyst was left feeling alone without any transference to uncover, analyze, and interpret. Only here and there were there signs of a transference process occurring. This hidden, soft, and diffuse transference situation made for confusing and uncertain countertransference feelings as well.

Klein established that the central conflict between love and hate runs through all development and shapes the individual's internal world (Stein 1990). Evidence of this fundamental fact can be extremely elusive with these types of patients and often camouflaged by extensive projective identification dynamics. Feldman (2004) has written about Betty Joseph's technical guidelines of showing interest in the moment-to-moment workings of the patient's internal world and the meanings behind the symptoms, acting out, and transference patterns. Discovering how the patient interferes with, hides from, or attacks new knowledge of self and others as well as containing this process and actively interpreting it helps the patient gradually internalize the analyst's therapeutic function. Feldman describes the importance of patiently containing, organizing, and verbalizing these in-the-moment interactions as they will gradually pave the way to helping the patient find the unconscious motives and phantasies that make them up. Betty Joseph has really emphasized the value of staying with how these matters are expressed in the interaction of the session. As Feldman has summarized (2004), she has refined Kleinian technique to the point of discovering how it can slow the analytic process down if the analyst combines too many descriptive observations with too many complicated explanatory interpretations.

I find this advice very helpful to follow, especially with more disturbed or anxious patients. First, one makes more in-the-moment descriptive interpretations and then gradually links those to the more explanatory level when the patient seems able to take them in. Sodre (2004) puts these ideas in his own words and notes how technically important it is to not interpret generalized transference patterns but to stick with the daily, current ways the patient moves towards or away, to the surface or to the depths, more concrete or more abstract, and more or less emotional towards the analyst in the clinical moment. He notes how we can become defensively lost in offering "because of" interpretations or historical reconstructions instead of clear descriptions of the actual therapeutic relationship and the way the patient uses us or does not use us in their ongoing phantasies and internal relational conflicts.

So, there can be a confusing, lengthy process in which the analyst may have to follow, contain, and understand the loud and hard transference states without having a full understanding of the entire clinical portrait.

CASE REPORT

Other times, a patient will present a much more quiet and soft transference which is also difficult to track and understand, but in another ways. David came to see me two years ago for help with his failing marriage. His angry and volatile wife had cheated on him. She told him she was sick of dealing with his health issues and tired of no sex in their relationship. David had suffered through prostate cancer, the treatment of it, and the aftermath of the treatment. He was also tremendously scared and anxious during this time and very focused on himself and his recovery. He developed impotency problems

along the way, which we explored as possibly a fear of not pleasing his angry
wife as well as a passive method of exacting revenge for her hurtful ways. After
his wife divorced him, he continued to work at his job as a park ranger, which
he loved. He hoped to one day become a park supervisor. His job did not pay
enough for him to have any savings and did not provide health insurance as
he was not a full-time worker. David also enjoyed writing short stories but
had not written in several years.

During the course of his analytic treatment, we explored the way he lived
life in an overly optimistic and passive manner, always avoiding conflict and
doing his best to please others even if it meant hiding or denying his own
desires. Over time, we discussed his upbringing, which included a very opin-
ionated father who became angry if someone didn't agree with him. David's
mother was a very passive woman who stayed in the background, trying to
please and smooth things out.

From the time when he was a small boy, David felt destined for greatness,
but this omnipotent phantasy was coupled with the castrating feeling of never
being clear about what he wanted to do with his life. He had many interests
and still does, but has never really settled into one thing that he excels at or
pursues with a passion. We have seen this as a way he circles around success
and power, but avoids it out of fear of conflict. An example is how David loves
writing short stories and sounds like he might be quite good at it. But, he has
never pursued it in a way that would give him a chance to find out.

In the transference, David has been very pleasant and forthcoming, always
attending on time and talking about what is on his mind. However, this has
created a sense of false consistency in the countertransference. I find myself
flowing along, feeling content with his reports of life, situations at work, and
his relationship with his new girlfriend. His health is fairly good now, his sex
life is pleasurable, and he receives compliments from his boss. So, I find myself relaxing in my chair as he lies on the analytic couch, both of us pleasantly
drifting down the stream. But, then I realize I feel we are being lazy, I am
not really interpreting much, and the treatment seems to be about nothing. I
regroup and find a scrap of interesting material here or there and a piece of
transference to comment on. But, we seem to still be lingering in a hazy, soft,
nothingness. There must be a transference, but I am not sure what it is or
where it is. David has anxiety and conflicts, but it is unclear exactly what they
are and where they come from. We are lost in the quiet fog together.

An example, in the second year of his analytic treatment, of how I found my way through this fog was when David told me a story of how he and his girlfriend were driving along and there was a slow-up in traffic. David honked the horn aggressively to get the person in front of him to let him by. His girlfriend was shocked at this sudden aggression and told him it scared her. He was completely confused about what she meant, and, after a long discussion, he still didn't see himself as being angry and didn't understand her reaction. In listening to his story, I was struck by how he was telling me of the slow driver in front of him and the traffic jam in a way that clearly conveyed the message of being fed up and angry. But, David would not own it outright. I told him he was giving me the anger in the story but then denying it in the discussion, just like he did with his girlfriend. He replied, "I don't think I am angry. Maybe it is because I am from New York! It is natural to honk and flip people off!"

I said, "You are telling me about how you reacted like your father in traffic, but you are telling me about it in a passive 'play it safe way' like your mother. You don't want me to think of you as not being nice. So, you sneak it in the story but don't own up to it in person. Maybe that is what threw your girlfriend off." David said he could see how that would make her confused and maybe scared, "but I don't want to be like my father." I said, "So, you have to act nice and keep things very smooth with me. You often tell me all about your day and what happened but rarely about your feelings, your reactions, and your wants. If we are smooth and conflict-free, we are OK. But, you are neutralized. You want to be a great writer and make your way up the ladder with your job at the park. But, it is rare that you tell me about these things with any passion or excitement. We are safe but smothered."

This line of interpretation was helpful and opened up a line of exploration that led to David talking more about his hopes and his fears of wanting more. He ended up working through some of his guilt and anxiety over competition and his fear of striving for success and power. He ended up telling me of how he didn't want any "flashy super success," just the good feeling of pursuing what really felt right to him, what felt exciting to him instead of anything he was supposed to like or pursue. But, this meant that he felt he was caught between pursuing what he wanted, a non-flashy goal that made him feel good or the more flashy goals he thought his girlfriend and others thought he should be pursuing.

The interesting and important fact here was that this meant that going with what he wanted looked like he was being lazy and unfocused when in fact he was content and happy but not sharing that with me or others out of fear of conflict or criticism. Here, we touched on him being worried about me being critical and not supportive of his own choices if they were different from mine. So, this was a shift in the soft, undefined transference to something in the moment that we were able to explore and slowly make sense of together. Together, we turned up the volume and clarity of the transference to something that was more understandable, something we could gain insight from, knowledge that could transform.

During a recent session, David walked in, lay down on the couch, and said, "So, where were we?" Many patients have presented themselves in this way at various times in their analysis. But, each transference and each set of projective identification efforts or assaults is always unique. So, depending on the unique mental fingerprint of that patient, I might respond by saying, "You having been thinking about us," "You have been drawn to what we discussed but also can't quite keep a hold of it," "You are trying to avoid free associating by rigidly continuing where we left off," or "You are worried that if you don't keep on track and instead just go with your own agenda I might be angry." With the quiet and soft nature of David's transference, I could easily fall into the countertransference response of simply telling him where I remember we left off and have him start talking in a general manner about that topic. Then, we could just meander down the lazy road of some vague and safe conversation that felt comfortable but that would avoid any meaningful exploration or risk on both our parts.

But, when I asked myself how was David using me or wanting to use me in that clinical moment, I felt he was suddenly being very passive and looking to me to take the lead, do the thinking, and decide what was important for him. So, I interpreted that he was asking me to take the lead and tell him what to do or say. I said, "You seem to want me to call the shots. I wonder why?"

Immediately, David associated to how his girlfriend has said on more than one occasion that she wishes he would be more assertive, find a better job, and act more responsible. David told me how recently she had told him about a job that seemed suited to him which she had found "on her own personal job search for David." He thought it indeed sounded like a promising job that he should look into but agreed with me when I pointed out how somehow she was really "calling the shots" and he seemed to stay in the shadows. I went on to interpret that perhaps he is anxious to call his own shots and show himself to me or his girlfriend as an assertive, direct man who knows what he wants. Indeed, I added that he has hinted around with me before about how he actually loves the job he has so in fact he may feel he is successful as is and doesn't want to look for another job. But, that might not please me or her if David thinks we want him to have a better-paying job with better health benefits and more prestige.

David agreed and began discussing the pros and cons of the job posting his girlfriend had found. It was located in Arizona, and David said, "Well, it is always so hot there that you have to stay inside all the time. I like that because if I have to stay inside, then I will be forced to sit down and write. As mentioned before, David had written short stories for many years and had a few published but never really pursued it in a way that would make him successful. At the same time, he had told me that writing was something he was "dearly passionate about and loved." I interpreted that he was guilty about pursuing things he loved and expressing his passions. Instead, he was more comfortable letting me and others take the lead and then there would be no conflict.

I said, "You want the hot Arizona weather to call the shots, not your own love of writing." We spent the rest of the session exploring this way he stayed in the shadows, denying his own identity, needs, and desires as a way to please others, avoid conflict, and not feel guilty. Here, we had established analytic contact (Waska 2007) and were actively exploring and working through the transference as well as his phantasies of self and other. The transference was now taking shape and was more accessible, not amorphous and seemingly without meaning. By carefully listening and looking for clues to David's projections, I was able to emerge from the haze of his usually quiet and soft transference, make helpful interpretations, and engage him on a much more meaningful manner than before. We probably will slip back into the soft, undefined, and lazy aspects of his quiet transference way of not relating, but we are finding our way out of that bog more often than not.

DISCUSSION

Roth (2001) has noted the value of tolerating the uncharted, unpaved path through this type of quiet, soft, and foggy transference to contain, gather, and slowly organize a language that best translates the patient's internal experiences. At the same time, she notes the importance of "level three and four" interpretations of the projective identification process the patient utilizes to draw the analyst into various phantasy interactions in which the analyst may end up enacting various internal object relationships with the patient.

So, I think that, while it is important to drift along for awhile in "level[s] one and two" (Roth 2001), interpretations about external objects and situations and occasional "me too" interpretations of the transference can also be enactments of a deliberate defensive or offensive effort by the patient to create a soft, lazy, hazy, and quiet transference in which everyone is happily unaware and can meander along in denial and complacency. Therefore, it is always important for the analyst to be on watch for such activity that can be camouflaged as the lack of activity. The more alert yet patient the analyst can be, the more he or she will be able to eventually notice occasional windows into more alive, meaningful feelings and thoughts that plague the patient.

Heimann (1956) discusses the importance of and mutative value of the transference interpretation. Modern Kleinians have come to the conviction that it is clinically vital to always be searching for, locating, understanding, and translating the transference. Heimann (1956) notes the value of always pondering why the patient is now doing what to whom in their phantasies, which then become acted out in the transference, through projective identification. She goes on to say that the tool of transference interpretation is not always available and indeed the analyst is often baffled. I believe this is most common when confronted with either the loud and sharp transference states or the quiet and soft transference profiles.

Feldman (1994) has pointed out how through projective identification, patients draw us into their most intense phantasies and use us in various ways to protect them from unbearable anxieties. When the patient succeeds in capturing us within this psychic envelope, we may feel lost and out of touch with the transference. We may end up feeling inadequate, persecuted from the patient's withholding and criticism, or depressed from a sense of analytic failure. We can end up feeling too full of the various toxic and unorganized projections or too empty from the patient's hoarding and hiding of personal feelings and thoughts. Bion (1959, 1962a, 1962b) has helped clinicians see the importance of being a container for the patient much as the good-enough mother needs to be for the struggling infant.

Feldman (1994) states that part of being an adequate container for the patient includes allowing ourselves to be affected by the distress of the patient as presented through acting out and projections. I would add that to be a proper container, we must allow ourselves to not know, but still learn as we go or even as we seem to become stagnant in the projective identification-induced countertransference. Feldman (1994) notes how helpful it is to not only allow ourselves to be drawn into enactments, without gross acting out, but also tolerating and recovering from our failures to contain or not act out as well as tolerating the intense thoughts and feelings that are often evoked in the transference/countertransference process.

I would add that we must learn to forgive ourselves for not knowing everything, for not being able to always locate the transference, and for not always knowing how to interpret the transference. This involves accepting the depressive position pain and loss of realizing the limits of our therapeutic abilities. By defensively avoiding the often confusing and frustrating search for the transference and the often difficult task of finding the best matching interpretations, the analyst colludes in the patient's projective invitation to sustain (Steiner 2000) the soft and quiet transference without interference or to sustain the loud, sharp, and chaotic transference without trying to learn about the moment-to-moment meaning of such an experience.

Consistent investigation of conscious fantasy and unconscious phantasy as well as the exploration of feelings and thoughts about other objects than the analyst can gradually give way to a portrait of the actual transference, an aspect of the defended transference, or a portion of the non-projected transference. When faithfully staying the course in this clinical manner, we usually end up rewarded by listening to what the patient has kept in hiding, not what they have eliminated through projection.

Finding the Meaning

Moment-to-Moment Transference Work with the Loud/Sharp States of Mind

Feldman (2004), reflecting Betty Joseph's approach to the clinical situation, reminds us of how important it is to understand exactly how the patient is using the analyst and utilizing, reacting, or attacking our interpretations. Some patients quickly solidify a loud, sharp, and colorful mode of transference which can be both a pushy advance into our minds and a desperate dive into the therapeutic envelope. Others maintain a silent, soft, and elusive mode of transference relating which creates an empty, lost, or limbo-type of nonconnection. In both cases, there is a significant use of projective identification to the degree that the analyst may not have a sense of what is really going on for weeks or months at a time. However, concentrated, moment-to-moment attention to the patient's phantasies and overall way of being with us can eventually breathe life and clarity into the analytic process.

One of the themes in Betty Joseph's work (1989) and her expansion of Melanie Klein's approach to understanding the mind is about helping the more disturbed patient, either paranoid (Klein 1946) or depressive (Klein 1935, 1940), to seek security and refuge in themselves. Most of our patients, especially our more difficult ones who bring us these loud or silent transference states, do not see themselves as a place of safety or compassion. Rather than be curious about their minds, their conflicts, and struggles and rather than believe they can learn from exploring themselves or come to a greater awareness, power, and joy, they see themselves as a dangerous object of investigation. Anger, punishment, guilt, loss, and emptiness are just some of the treacherous states they are convinced lie in wait for them if they begin to know themselves. So, knowledge is contaminated by the dramatic conflicts between love and hate. Indeed, knowledge is often the first victim of these phantasies of corrupted love and hate between self and other.

However, Betty Joseph advocates ongoing efforts by the analyst to clarify and organize the patients' most immediate emotional experiences so they can hopefully begin to recognize, acknowledge, and re-own previously rejected aspects of self. By way of interpretations, we help the patients understand what they are emotionally going through. In this highly descriptive manner that highlights the transference and whatever defenses may be most operational at that moment, the analyst is demonstrating how they themselves are not only able to tolerate, contain, and survive those states, but that they are actually interested in them and see them as a vehicle of valuable learning, growth, and ultimately healing. Joseph (1989) believes this descriptive, inviting, and exploratory stance will eventually be internalized by the patients, and while initially the analyst may be doing most of the work towards integration, gradually the patients take on these tasks. Only at this point is it helpful to start adding interpretations regarding motive, historical impacts, and explanatory formulations. Otherwise, a premature move in this direction can be intellectual and defensive at best and experienced as a betrayal or attack at worst. Of course, listening closely to the patients' reactions to our interpretations can reveal how helpful or hurtful our comments are.

With patients who have the more loud, confusing, and sharp transferences as well as the patients who have silent, soft, or seemingly unreachable transferences, this Kleinian approach is even more important to use in a patient, here-and-now fashion.

CASE #1

Sally was all things at all times. She was needy, demanding, weak, passive, insightful, naive and simpleminded, overly trusting, withdrawn and withholding, seductive, and off-putting. The transference was loud and sharp as well as confusing, complex, and very hard to define. However, over time we made sense of it as well as the anxious phantasies that make it up. But, this was only possible when I was able to anchor my countertransference in tolerance, curiosity, and the commitment to knowing more over time without giving up or expecting too much.

Sally came to me at age forty. She was depressed and said she "felt like life had passed her by and she was left with an empty sack of nothing while the rest of the world seemed to be having relationships, families, and finding happiness." Sally had spent the last twenty years moving around the country from one sales job to another, always "hoping to meet Mr. Right but never fitting in or finding anything. I have always been on this meaningless loop, and when I get sick of it, I just move. Now that I am forty, I think I realize I can't do that anymore. I could, but it doesn't seem to help anything. I need help, Doc!"

This last remark was a sharp and anxious transference moment in which she pressured me for immediate gratification, attention, and service. This came out as a plea for help, a desperate rush for answers, and a run for safety. But, it was also a "hop to it" sort of demand for me to be her magical pill that would make everything go away so she would suddenly feel all better and new. I interpreted these states of mind but Sally was very concrete about it and told me "of course that is what she wanted and didn't see anything wrong with that." I replied that she seemed very upset over not knowing herself and the feeling of being so empty inside. I said that if we merely tried to come up with a magical Band-Aid to make it all go away, we would be ignoring her and not giving her any value. I thought this transference moment was a repetition of her own rejection of self and possibly her memories of feeling rejected by others. My interpretation seemed to make her less anxious, and she seemed a bit interested in learning more about herself.

Sally told me about her past and said she thought it had a lot to do with her "current dead-end." She described being "the fat kid" growing up and how everyone at school teased her and avoided her. Sally said she felt happy and OK about herself but that everyone else's view of her corroded that and left her "feeling ugly and broken." Here, it seemed she was indicating a split of some sort between good and bad and inside and outside.

A nearby neighbor woman befriended Sally and encouraged Sally to exercise and diet. But, this woman's husband also took an interest in Sally. He started making sexual advances, telling Sally she was pretty and that he was in love with her. Sally was sixteen, and he was thirty. Over the course of the next three years, they had a secret relationship which included sex. He spent hours telling her about his sexual fantasies, his marital troubles, and his personal problems. During the first year of this clandestine relationship, he pursued her. But, after they began having sex, he played it cool and seemed to not want to be with her except for sex. Sally felt rejected and pursued him. She spied on him, followed him around, and tried to connect with him for that magical love and attention he seemed to initially provide.

Sally told me she felt happy that she had a boyfriend just like all her other friends in college did and only later realized the predatory nature of it all. In fact, this man eventually was sent to jail for having sex with an underage girl, and he apparently had a long history of such behavior. Sally now feels angry, hurt, and humiliated that she was used and betrayed in these ways. She thinks that her self-image as a fat, unwanted girl and the effects of this man's advances have impacted her and have influenced her current troubles with men. This seemed to indicate a positive and healthy ability to reflect and evaluate herself in a holistic manner. However, this insight quickly slipped away and was replaced with more of an enactment of these feelings and memories.

So, in the transference and extra-transference, I noticed a parallel to her story of being pursued by an older man and then in turn her frantically pursuing him. Almost immediately after I expressed some curiosity about her feelings and conflicts, Sally started pushing for "answers" and "solutions." She said she wanted to find out what was getting in the way of her "having a good life, living a normal life just like everyone else her age." She told me she "was sick of always finding half-baked men who are broken in some way and need fixing. They are never fully functioning, and I spend my time trying to fix them, hoping that they will one day turn into the man I want, but it never happens. They just stay in their sorry state, and I stay lonely and angry."

I interpreted that she was saying this in a rushed, impatient manner that seemed to speak to her frustration or anger at me for not giving her what she wanted when she wanted. I added that she might be feeling anxious and desperate to find some shelter from her sense of being lost and unloved. This was in line with Melanie Klein's (1928) ideas regarding the early and primitive desires to scoop out mother's breast and greedily own the contents. But, this creates a broken, victimized object that is then internalized and leads to a projective identification cycle of feeling victimized and unfairly ignored along with a sense of demand and criticism aimed at both self and others.

This cycle increases paranoid-schizoid anxieties (Klein 1946) and prevents the normal progress to the depressive position (Klein 1935, 1940) by which there is a growing sense of self, "I-ness" and "you-ness" (Grotstein 1982). This individuation and independence will normally unfold within phantasies of self and object that create a sense of balance and integration. Sally was not able to reach this internal place and was left struggling to grab what she felt to be withheld and denied.

This pull on me to produce the answers that would fix her and relieve her "broken" status continued for the first few months. I did my best to contain it, not act out my countertransference responses to it, and to gradually and consistently interpret it for what I saw to be the immediate edge of anxiety and phantasy at that given clinical moment. Sometimes, it was her treating me like a gumball machine, impatiently waiting for her next candy to roll into her hands. Other times, it was a plea to end her suffering and help her find a way to join the human race. In general, it was the phantasy of being left out and not knowing how to obtain the level of connection she wanted and longed for with a man.

There was a great deal of back and forth within the transference with Sally. She would proclaim something one week and then highlight the opposite the following week. When she talked about how hard she worked and the countless hours she put in with virtually no time off, I asked her why she subjected herself to what sounded like a narrow, unsatisfying lifestyle from her description. She would tell me, "I love the pace! It is gratifying to travel, jetting here or there, and see new places, meet new people, and create new business. I just want to meet a man who is also involved that way, going to meetings, part of the corporate lifestyle, on the go."

This was part of a way Sally related to me that left me feeling that she was superficial and only after money and appearance. I made that interpretation and suggested that she was uncomfortable searching deeper for what she was really about and what she really might want out of life. She said she has never thought much about it, that she simply looked around for a man and a job that paid well, and when things didn't go right, she moved. Indeed, Sally had a history of moving around the country and from city to city. Initially, she talked about this with pride and a sense of disdain for others who "were stuck in a rut." She basically discarded people and places when she didn't find what she was looking for, hoping for, and dreaming of. But, then after she moved and realized things were just the same, she became depressed and felt "very empty inside." Then and now, she was angry that she was "stuck in a rut."

The loud and sharp transference states that emerge in psychoanalytic treatment impact the analyst. With Sally, she seemed to push this moving-whenever-things-got-painful-or-disappointing aspect of her story into me, which left me feeling a bit anxious and worried that it was only a matter of time before she found me unworthy, another man she would walk away from. I made this interpretation, and Sally told me, "I think I have learned that is a strategy that doesn't work. So, I think I will be around. But, I do think of leaving when I realize how expensive it is to live here and how stuck I feel. I wish I could just move back home to be around my family." This yearning to be back home as a pampered child with her parents came up a great deal, and over time my sense of it was that she literally wished to be back home as a child and feel exactly like she used to before she ever moved out to go to college. So, it seemed we were up against this idealized blissful reunion phantasy that surely looked better than having to grow up, find her own identity, and seek out a relationship in which she was not a victim, stalker, or nursemaid.

When Sally resorted to the "give me answers now" way of being desperate and pushy for help, I felt heckled and bothered. For awhile, it felt irritating, and I wanted to tell her to be quiet and calm down. This was interesting as I was being drawn to ignoring her and telling her that her anxiety was simply irritating. However, by containing this and exploring it within the counter-transference, it gradually came to me that her beating the drum for help was part of how she in fact made herself feel empty and desperate. At one point, I said, "You sound so desperate for help. You want me to help you right now and tell you what is wrong right now! But, do you even know what you actually want help with?"

Here, I was confronting her manic grabbing at something and really not knowing what she was after, why she was after it, or what might happen if she found whatever it was she was grabbing for. In response, Sally said, "Well, I just want to feel better. I don't want to be so miserable." And then she fell silent. I said, "So, you want to escape this empty nothingness and loneliness so much that you want me to immediately give you something to fill it up with or a dressing for the painful wound. But, we really don't know what this emptiness is or where the pain comes from. Just trying to change it to something else, we are ignoring you and what is really happening inside of you. If we notice there is a crater inside of you and desperately try and fill it up, that might feel better for awhile but there is still a hole there. Maybe we can find out how that hole got there and why it remains there. Then, maybe we will know what is best to do or not do about it."

Here, in my interpretations, I was acting as a container for her anxieties and pointing in a new direction where we both might find some answers that could last and that could heal, not merely mask or distract. However, this type of intense and desperate dynamic so common with the louder transference states creates a sharp and jumpy countertransference condition in which the analyst is prone to getting swept up in the projective identification process and prone to act out these panic feelings with the patient by trying to dress things up with immediate answers, behavioral prescriptions, advice, medication, or manic interpretations.

Sally would make things feel very complicated and confusing by abruptly switching her allegiances. She would tell me a story about how she wanted to travel and live the fast paced busy corporate life and meet a rich lawyer or doctor who also had a busy, important practice. Then, they could meet up for late night dinners and dash off together in the morning to their important meetings. At first I noticed myself reacting to this story with some disdain. I thought of Sally as naïve, stupid, and greedy. She seemed to only want immediate superficial gratification. But, after a while, I also realized this was like the fancy idea a young child or immature teenager might have of what awaits them in the adult world. It was simplistic and caricatured, without much depth or reality, but an earnest attempt of a child to grasp what lies ahead and what excitement might be in store.

Here, I was brought back to the early sexual experiences she had with the predatory neighbor. From Sally's recollections, it was as if he tried to pretend they were a normal couple, two young lovers. She liked this and wanted to pretend along with him, seeking this idealized couple phantasy and his complete acceptance and attention. However, it was soon after that he acted uninterested to manipulate her into pursuing him. Then, she felt shunned and ignored except for when he decided he was ready for a sexual encounter. So, Sally had to pursue him most of the time and ended up feeling unwanted and not important.

This flip-flop appeared in how Sally related to me. After the sessions in which she told me she loved the busy, corporate life with fast paced, important meetings and travel, she came in looking exhausted and told me she was "fed up with flying everywhere and living out of a suitcase." Now, Sally said she was worn out and tired of being stuck "in the grind." I interpreted that perhaps she had been trying to keep herself happy in this manic way, seeing herself as successful and important, but now she was facing what she really felt inside, tired and lonely. I also mentioned this in relation to the transference as some of her traveling had interfered with our meetings.

She said, "Actually, when I am not here, I do some of my own thinking and I have learned a great deal. I have figured out a few things about how my past has influenced my current way of living." She went on to discuss some important reflections and insights that showed she was indeed not always naïve, confused, and simple. I thought that this was an important sign of her feeling she could relate to me as a different kind of woman, a smart, independent one who was capable of showing herself care and attention. I said this and mentioned that she might be able to depend on me without giving up her own identity.

Sally replied, "Well, maybe. But, I don't think I am capable of doing that with someone I want to date. As a matter of fact, I am still hanging out with this loser that I feel is my best friend." Sally was referring to a man she had been dating for a year and was constantly disappointed in him. She told me how she was initially intrigued by his kindness and openness. He was a bartender, and she thought that if she helped him for long enough, he would become motivated to go back to school, get a better job, and become a boyfriend she could trust and look up to. But, after a year of this attempted makeover, she felt angry and frustrated because he was still the "same old loser."

I was struck by how she would describe moments in which this man seemed to genuinely care for her and spend time with her but then Sally would become upset that he couldn't offer her "the whole package," meaning a better job, commitment, and so forth. Even though she had threatened to leave him for some time now, she had not been able to part with him.

I interpreted that she divided men into the perfect "whole packages" that she felt she never deserved and the broken-in-need-of-repair variety of men whom she felt comfortable with and trusted, only to then feel betrayed and disappointed in. Here, I was interpreting her splitting of the rescuing object with the rescued object, and the hoped-for change into an ideal, perfect object shifting to feeling taken advantage of and left with a malfunctioning bad object. Her associations led Sally to talk about her guilt over about letting go of the broken man, feeling scared she would never find anyone better because she felt broken herself, and that somehow she didn't deserve the whole package.

I interpreted that she was hoping I would help her find this perfect object but I would only end up being another disappointment because this was the phantasy of an ideal object that didn't exist. She was in fact reluctant to show me who she was currently, on the inside, and to struggle with creating a whole package that was truly her and not a magical composite of ideal rescuers and rescues. I said that part of this was facing how important and soothing her experience with this man was, even if he wasn't someone she was going to spend her life with. By discarding the sensitive, valuable moments with him in which she felt genuinely understood, she left herself to be an empty shell searching for temporary pleasures that quickly faded.

Sally responded, "It is very hard to just accept his caring without feeling I need to be with him forever in this disappointing way or to tell him to hurry up and give me all the rest."

In her efforts at finding a "better package," Sally came in and told me about how she had been excited to meet a man at a work function and he "seemed to be educated, rich, and very interesting." He had suggested they go out to dinner together and enjoy some of his special wines he had recently acquired. But, he later told Sally that the restaurant was asking a high corkage fee so perhaps they should consider having dinner at her place to save that unnecessary expense.

Now, when Sally told me this, I noticed her lack of concern about the situation. I thought him wanting to have dinner at her place under that premise was a bad sign, given she said he was well off financially and therefore shouldn't have cared about paying a corkage fee. It seemed like a fairly thinly disguised ruse to be in her house instead of a restaurant, which seemed either sleazy or slightly scary. In the countertransference, I was surprised at how stupid or naïve Sally seemed and I felt like telling her to wake up and smell the coffee.

I used this feeling to try and understand something more about how Sally operated with her objects. After reflecting on this information, I interpreted that she had high hopes that this man would prove to be a "winner" instead of a "loser." She said, "I am just having a casual dinner and drink with him. We will see how it goes." Here, I felt like stepping in as her father and warning her about being with this man. It seemed that in her desires to have more, she was turning her own common sense off and giving it to me. I tried to contain and understand this projective identification dynamic better instead of enacting it.

To do this, I had to sit on my countertransference reactions to Sally's wanting an object to be a certain ideal way so much that she appeared to be putting herself on the sacrificial altar. I certainly wondered if this was a repeat of her experience with the older man when she was a teen. When she came back for the next session, Sally told me she "was shocked at how it all turned out." When the man came over to her place, he ended up drinking quite a bit of her wine, became drunk, and tried to have sex with Sally. She kept telling him it was getting late and she needed to get up early for work. Eventually, that worked. She had to call him a cab, and he said he forgot his wallet, so she had to pay for the cab.

Sally cried as she said, "I can't believe how he acted. I thought we were going to have a casual friendly get together, and he assumed it was a date and would sleep over. What is wrong with me that I end up meeting all the weird ones?"

I interpreted that perhaps she wanted him to be the "whole package" so much that she quickly looked away from all the clues that showed he wasn't. She would rather gamble that he might be different than what he seems or that she could somehow change him into what she wants than to have to realize he was not going to give her the type of love and attention she craved.

Sally replied, "I think I am really stupid that way. I completely put on the blinders. At the same time, he did say it was because of the expensive corkage fee at the restaurant." I said, "You want me to be the one with common sense and tell you off for not realizing he is either really cheap or just wanted to have an excuse to be in your home on the first date. It sounds like you want me to be the voice of reason and to also protect you."

Sally responded, "I have a part in this too. I get so excited about getting what I want that I decide to gamble on all the rest." I said, "It is really different for you to stop and look at your contribution and own it. But now, in this moment, you realize you have more of a conscious choice in all these things, which means you don't have to feel like a victim to loser men." She said, "We will see." Here, she broke free of her normal state of aggressive desire, denial, and projection and was able to own her manipulation of the object and the consequences of that control. She suddenly had more freedom and autonomy instead of being the victim and the lonely one.

From the point of view of Hanna Segal (1983) and her Kleinian contributions to the field, Sally is suffering from narcissistic conflicts regarding the inability to love herself and to allow a vision of herself being loved by her objects. Instead, she puts a lid on how much she deserves and how much the object is capable of giving. Then, in retaliation for this lack of abundance, she searches out the ideal object that can give her the phantasy of what she remembers at home with her family and friends, an ideal "loving time with acceptance and support at all times." As Segal points out, the narcissistic patient, through projective identification and splitting, tries to control, own, and tunnel into an object that is both idealized and degraded. Sally was always on the verge of bliss but then rudely disappointed.

The Kleinian technique involves close interpretive interaction with the patient as they cycle through the paranoid and depressive aspects of these unconscious phantasies. This type of transference, as illustrated in the case of Sally, is loud, jagged, and gripping, yet scattered and without containment or integration. Therefore, the analyst feels they are being taken on a colorful roller-coaster ride without any known destination.

These types of projective identification and splitting mechanisms left Sally with ongoing problems in the area of separation. She demonstrated a severe difficulty around separation from her desired objects and often felt betrayed, forgotten, and cut off from the magically soothing breast of her phantasies. This was in turn projected onto me, and I was sometimes caught up in the countertransference side of this. When Sally would not attend her sessions due to work conflicts and traveling, she sometimes came back to tell me that she "had realized much and learned a lot without me. Thinking of things on her own and talking with friends had made her come to important insights. She learned a few things that were new and very helpful."

What she went on to tell me about was indeed important and showed how she did not attack herself or eliminate knowledge all the time. So, there was progress being made and independent thinking. But, it felt like it was in spite of me. I felt forgotten, unwanted, or lacking in value. I tried to sit with these feelings and not act them out, doing my best to understand what seemed like a manic response to separation and loss.

Brenman (1982) states that the patient may act out, may feel incredibly and unbearably jealous, and may resort to denial and manic attacks on the lost object. Sally had been trying to separate from the man she had been trying to nurse and transform for over a year. Whenever she did create space between the two of them or when he didn't call for a week, she was upset and jealous. Even though she vowed that she didn't want a relationship with him and "didn't want to have sex with him since he might be seeing other women," she checked his phone for evidence of calls to other women. Of course, when he did come around and showed her attention, she put him down and felt used and suffocated but also seemed to melt when he showed the smallest measure of care and support.

Also, Sally made numerous references to wanting to move back to the city where she grew up and where her parents lived. She longed for the "apple pie home town goodness and how people there understood her and her family loved her." But, she didn't think she could ever return there because the older man, who was arrested for having sex with underage girls, was still living there and was now out of jail. Sally was scared that he might "do something" to her, and she was worried she might be so angry if she saw him that she might hurt him. So, here again the ideal union with her hometown was made into a sad and persecutory separation. This was the cycle of a quest for an ideal union followed by a disappointing contact with a bad or broken object she would be burdened by while everyone else seemed to have found the pot of gold at the end of the rainbow.

Betty Joseph, as reported by Feldman (2004), has highlighted the clinical importance of assessing and understanding exactly how a patient uses us and shapes us as their particular object at particular times in the treatment. The patient's immediate defenses and anxieties as well as their pattern of desires and needs are lived out in how they try to move towards or away from the analyst's mind, the analyst's interpretations, and the analytic relationship. Also, Joseph is unique in emphasizing the importance of evaluating the patient's acceptance of a loving object that is supportive and promotes change, learning, and growth. Most of our patients work vigorously against such a stimulating, healing object even though they angrily lament its absence. But, when faced with the presence of such an object, in the guise of the analyst, they often turn away in fear, envy, or spite. Sally demonstrated most of these psychic conflicts with her male objects.

After discussing the "wine incident" with the man she had over to her home, Sally was leaving my office and asked me, "Do you like wine?" I asked her what she was thinking about. She said, "Well, I just thought if you like wine, maybe I will bring you a bottle next time since I have that case I bought from my brother that I told you about. We could even do a trade if you like it." I was taken by surprise and felt intruded on and violated, like she was trying to seduce me and break through my boundaries. It was an exact repeat of what just happened to her with the date. Sally had gone into great detail telling me about how this man got drunk, tried to kiss her numerous times, kept drinking her wine that she had bought from her brother, and went "way beyond any appropriate norms."

I thought that Sally was setting up the same situation, only now with her as predator and me as possible victim. Just as I thought she was using projective identification to have me be the voice of reason and parental protection in telling her to watch out for this man, I thought she was now inviting me to be the trustworthy father with boundaries instead of the child-molesting neighbor man. I also remembered how Sally told me that she gets so excited and eager to get what she wants that she puts aside her own knowledge and self-containment. She trades in her respect for herself or others in exchange for the chance of an ideal love and perfect attention.

So, I interpreted, "You are thinking of us being together in a similar way as that guy. You are hopeful we would be friendly and the wine would just be a nice gesture. But, it looks like you are inviting me to either step over some boundaries or remind you of where we stand with each other. I wonder if you think the only way to get closer is to put yourself at risk or to forget about the boundaries." Sally said, "Oh, I see. So, you don't think it would be good to do a trade?" We were at the end, so I had no time to really respond. I simply said, "It is hard for you to look at the details of how you relate and learn from them. Let's look at that next time."

Predictably, she never brought it up again until I did, and she said she didn't see much wrong with it but "understood, if that was my policy." I asked her if she is offended that I am blocking her from being closer to me in this whine-for-attention way. Sally said, "I guess I just wasn't sure how you operated. I wanted to ask you about your vacation and where you went last week. I hope you had a good time. Maybe you like going to the beach just like I do. But, I didn't ask you because I know the rules prevent you from answering anything about yourself." I said she seemed to like the idea that we were similar and had the same interests. I also asked how she had come up with "the rules" since I never mentioned anything like that. Sally told me she "just assumed those were the rules so she didn't ask.

Then, Sally said, "My last therapist hugged me, and we talked lots about his life. He told me about his unhappy marriage and what he did for fun." I asked her how she reacted to that. Sally told me, "In the beginning, it was exciting and interesting. I felt like I had a front row seat into his personal drama. So, I guess I ignored the feelings that something was amiss. But, after a few sessions, I felt like he should be paying me to cry on my shoulder! And, he started to give me hugs at the end of each session which felt good but I didn't really see how they fit in to the whole thing. So, after about six sessions, when he only talked about his lousy marriage and gave me a big hug, I stopped going."

I said, "So, you like the front-row-seat feeling with men but then end up feeling used and empty. Maybe we don't have to do that. Maybe instead we can understand how you do want change but the pull of that old excitement gets in the way of change." Sally said, "I like that. When do we start?" I said, "You are discounting the fact that we have been doing that from day one. When you do that, you make us into broken empty packages instead of trusting that we are good packages or broken packages that are being repaired." She replied, "I get it."

Then, I interpreted that she seemed to try and see me as someone without rules, hence the wine gift, the trading wine for therapy, and her general friendly nature at times. But, I added that she seemed glad I was forced to follow "the rules." Sally told me, "I think I know what you mean. I want to find a man who can give me everything I want, but I end up opening the floodgates and who knows what the hell might come floating in!" Here, Sally allowed for another moment of insight and allowed herself to look at herself and her objects in a new, less distorted manner that produced some learning and healing.

Often in this initial three-month period of treatment, I was left with a state of confusion and scatteredness regarding what exactly was going on with Sally and what the exact nature of her transference and phantasy state was. This is common with patients who exhibit a louder and sharp style of transference and projective identification relating. However, by utilizing the Kleinian method and following Betty Joseph's close attention to the here-and-now interaction that had been taking place in each session, I was able to begin having a gradual sense of what Sally was struggling with. I was left with two provisional impressions of how she related to herself and to her objects and the possible nature of her anxieties and desires.

I think Sally was constantly searching for an ideal, attentive man who would mend her, fix her, and take care of her. To do this, he would have to be someone she could look up to, admire, and respect in a very special way. But, I think Sally's need, desire, and demand was very strong and she felt both aggressively eager to obtain it and then guilty about whether she deserved it, given how broken and ugly she felt about herself.

This sense of self-hatred was projected and instead of her feeling broken and in need of repair, she found herself seeking out men who seemed broken and in need of special attention and compromised attachment. So, the allure of attention, love, and being transformed from a fat, broken, unwanted girl to a strong, lovable, important woman was so great that she attacked her own knowledge, common sense, and ability to assess others in the hopes of getting what she wanted immediately and perfectly.

This dynamic seemed to be interwoven with another deep phantasy that flavored her transference. I had the impression that Sally, even though she never mentioned it within this short period of treatment, wanted her parents to have noticed that something was quite wrong. Sally never mentioned this, and I noticed that I had not given it any thought either until several months into the treatment. This was a glaring empty spot that I think she felt unconsciously but did not want to explore because of the intense feelings that surrounded it.

Specifically, I think she was constantly hoping someone, starting with her parents and now her analyst, would notice her being in the midst of dangerous or hurtful situations and warn her, rescue her, or protect her. But, by waiting for me to step in and advise her and protect her, she had to be vulnerable and weak, a potential victim just hoping for the kindness of a stranger. But, then through projective identification, the kind stranger phantasy turned into strange stranger who is either unkind or unavailable.

This interlocked with another aspect of the transference in which the roles of predator and victim were projected back and forth onto her objects, including her analyst. Sally would be the demanding, "I want the answers now," "I want a good man with style and money right now," type of bully who looks down on the broken men she dated and her slow-to-cure-her analyst. She was the hard driven, corporate dynamo who knew how to seal the deals and work the meetings, carving out a reputation and feeling powerful. So, in these ways, I was the victim, the slow and broken-down man, and she was the pursuer, the dominator.

But, Sally also felt victimized by the older man of her teens, by the various men she dated as an adult for never giving her what she needed, by her analyst for not providing the healing advice quick enough to stop her pain, and by a culture that demanded women be high-powered, driven winners.

Bit by bit, we are proceeding in our analytic journey toward understanding and healing. For patients such as Sally, this can be a difficult and rocky task as they present a loud and sometimes jarring transference that can be hard to define and work with. The analyst can easily become lost in trying to overly define the transference or pin it down prematurely. If, instead, the analyst can stick with the most immediate nature of the projective identification process and the moment-to-moment transference process, a gradual working-through is possible which slowly may reveal the wider theme operating.

Bion's (1962a, 1962b) work refining Klein's discovery of projective identification has highlighted the importance of containment in analytic work, especially with more scattered and difficult-to-reach patients such as Sally. Part of the difficulty Sally seemed to have was with a corrupted sense of self-containment in which she attacked her own containing function, only allowing others to contain her. But, even that was temporary before she seemed to discard the object's organizing function of containment in order to seek out a more desperate, demanding way of being with herself and others.

In discussing the Kleinian understanding of projective identification, Steiner (1998) points out how the process is often used as a method of communication but more troubled patients can use it to attack, destroy, or control the object, sometimes provoking countertransference reactions. When Sally projected her predator/victim dynamic which was blended with her broken and needy rescue-and-repair dynamic, I often felt pushed to tell her, "You broken fool, wake up and take a look around."

Here, I could see how I was now the aggressive bully attacking the poor victim while she looked to me at the same time to be the wise, protecting parent who showed her the way and enlightened her. But, this shift from benign to malignant was a common thread in how she related to herself and others. In trying to gradually understand her phantasies and interpret them in the moment-to-moment therapeutic interaction, I was offering Sally a chance to develop symbolic functioning instead of her concrete acting out. One of our goals was to establish thinking and understanding.

Part of the Kleinian approach to containment includes the idea that the patient may attempt to abuse the containing object, overfilling it and expelling into it without regard for the object. If the analyst does nothing but accept this attack and this greedy dumping, the patient may easily internalize an injured, malfunctioning container unable to protect itself. By setting interpretive limits in the analytic situation, the analyst helps demonstrate a reliable, strong container that can demand respect while offering help and psychological embrace. So, when I set limits with Sally's offer of wine as a gift and a trade, I was saying no to her seductive, aggressive transference move and in that sense did not allow myself to be used as she felt used when a teen or now as an adult. I showed myself to be a different sort of object, one that could protect myself as well as still want to be with her without attacking her in revenge or sulking off in self-pity and resentment.

Rey (1988) has written about how patients bring their damaged objects to treatment so they can find a way to repair them and undo the damage they have caused them. The patient hopes we can save or restore the damaged or dying objects that they carry with them. They look to us for this reparation as they feel they cannot find a way to resuscitate their objects. Sally felt surrounded by broken objects that she felt compelled to please, heal, and cater to. This guilt was primitive and persecutory (Grinberg 1964) and led to her limiting her own learning, growth, or difference from the object. Her guilt left her feeling compelled to put herself in limbo for the magical day when her objects rose up from the dead and became the wonderful men she dreamed of and felt she deserved. But, when this never happened, she was angry and hurt, lashing out and demanding better, which left her ultimately guilty again and sure she was worthless and deserving nothing.

Spillius (1983) has noted that Kleinians utilize the concept of the death instinct clinically. She explains how Kleinian analysts track the patient's attacks on life and on the good object as a result of deep envy and the anxiety of life, change, and difference. She notes how the death instinct can often become part of a destructive projective identification cycle. I believe this was part of Sally's psychic struggle in which she projected the dying or dead object and then felt obligated to save and repair but was furious to have to stay with the dying object rather than to be able to pursue the good or ideal objects others seemed to own.

Segal (1993a) has also spoken about the clinical usefulness of the death instinct concept. She extends Freud and Klein in noting how all humans from birth have needs which are never being met in the ideal, immediate way we wish for. In reaction, there are two responses, and some patients rely pathologically on one or the other. We seek satisfaction for our needs and accept the frustrations, loss, guilt, conflicts, and anxieties that go along with that pursuit. This is the life instinct which leads to object seeking, love, and care for others. Or, we try to annihilate the need, both in ourselves and in the object of our need. This is the death instinct, and it leads to aggression, envious attacks, withdrawal, and avoidance.

Grotstein (1977) has developed the idea that the death instinct can be a part of a biological warning system that helps the individual when confronted by predator/prey situations. The individual has a built-in warning system and reacts to protect itself or others by attacking the source of predator threat, even if it seems to be one's own self and one's own desires. In other words, the death instinct, while in healthy development can assist in protecting ourselves and those we love, in pathology, it becomes the assassin that hunts us or our loved ones in order to eliminate all perceived wrongs and predicted threats.

Grotstein (1985) goes on to say the death instinct, when operating in a healthy manner, creates the urge for protection and reparation as well as a method to drive out the bad object so as to be back with the good object. It is a message to the mother/analyst to step in and help rid the bad object so that the infant/patient can find union with the good object once again. In all these ways, Sally seemed to rely on the death instinct to communicate, defend, and attack herself and her objects when they were not up to her standards. It was these standards that I tried to gain more detailed understanding of in the heat of the clinical moment.

Rosenfeld (1974) has noted that the Kleinian method involves not trying to discover the patient's most deeply disturbing unconscious conflicts but rather the most immediate anxiety that has conscious, pre-conscious, and unconscious components and to interpret the cutting edge of that anxiety as it unfolds in the moment-to-moment, here-and-now transference and phantasy work. It is this close and current focus that helps build analytic contact (Waska 2007).

In a recent session, Sally told me how after going to Hollywood for a wedding for a friend, she came back hopeful and ready to "live life." She described how she felt she had "finally found a place where the people were just like her, the weather was just right, the vibes are good, and men who seem to have it going on were interested in me." She said, "The neighborhoods are good, the rental market is better, and the beaches are great. I fit in and everyone seems to have reached a good level of success and happiness."

In the countertransference, I felt a sense of disdain for Sally, looking down on her for being so superficial and naïve. When she started talking about moving there and "having found her place," I found myself feeling angry and cast aside. She had found the answer to her problems. It was not internal and in the realm of our relationship. It was external and waiting for her in Hollywood. Here, I think she was killing off the chance to breathe life into her empty existence because facing her internal conflicts was so daunting and relationships seemed so unpredictable that she would rather hook herself up to an artificial respirator in which external factors made her feel alive and her manic hope seemed invincible.

I kept a watchful eye on my countertransference during this period of treatment as countertransference is always both an essential tool to understand the nature of projective identification processes at work as well as a method of managing a balance between containment and enactment. These ideas are part of what Pick (1985) considers the Kleinian embracing of the total or complete countertransference (Waska 2010c) which is considered an unavoidable but often helpful or even crucial element of the overall analytic treatment process.

So, after Sally spoke of her new place in paradise, I said it must be a disappointment to come back to her home town, to me and all the other men in this less than ideal place. She said, "Well, I am glad to see you again, but when I went over to visit Oscar (the man she kept trying to break it off with), I was shocked. He is now living in a grotesque roommate situation with three other losers, and I think they are all alcoholics. I had never been there before, and when I went in, the whole place reeked of booze and cigarettes. His room was a small shithole that smelled and was dirty. His mattress did not even have sheets on it! I was overwhelmed. I cannot believe I let myself fall for this guy. He has absolutely no motivation in life and is obviously going nowhere. I have wasted so much time on him. But, this was a really good wake-up call. The last straw was the other night when he spent the night with me. We do not have sex because I don't trust that he hasn't slept around and has some nasty bug. But, when he got up in the morning, he wanted to wash his clothes in my sink because those are the only clothes he has and they were dirty. I was so appalled."

I interpreted that even though he seems like such a failure, there is something very comforting and inviting about him that keeps drawing her back and making it difficult for her to figure out what she really wants and what action to take. Here, I was interpreting the idea that when projective identification is used in excess, the object is needed as they are now the repository for so much of the patient's internal world. The link between the two is made even more dramatic by the intense projections. I said, "You really need him in some ways but really feel trapped by what you see in him too." Sally started crying and said, "It is so hard to let go. I do need him in some sick way. If I dump him, I feel bad and guilty that he will just end up on the streets or something. But, worse than that, I am scared I will be single again and all alone. No one will want me. I feel so fat and ugly. No one will ever want me."

I interpreted how Sally needs a bad object, a broken object to use as a prop to feel better, nursing it to health like she would like to be rescued. She feels this broken object is as good as she will ever do, so she must hang onto it even though she quickly feels the special ideal magic and attention fade to black. She would rather feel chained to the bad object than to feel adrift with no object at all. Sally responded by telling me she would dump him but she can't stand the thought of letting him be with another woman. She said, "I can't bear the thought of him having sex with someone else, so I need to keep him close and in my sight even though I think he is disgusting." She added that she felt the same way about the older man when she was a teen, that she hated the fact he was married and later hated that fact that he was having sex with other teens.

Here, I thought that Sally was describing her struggle with envy and the resulting feeling of desperation for the love the object had but only seemed willing to give under sadistic, conditional ways. Her desire for control and ownership of the object as a shield against a paranoid sense of loss and desolation combined with the primitive pull of the death instinct to make a constrictive glass ceiling under which she could only have crumbs and broken pieces of love, but never the entire plate. With these thoughts in mind, I interpreted that she needed to keep her men on short leashes so that she had ownership and didn't lose her companion.

Sally replied, "It is the once-in-a-blue-moon moment when Oscar is sober and caring that I live for. I wait for that. It is like wonderful magic." I interpreted that she feels she must keep him on a leash and under her control so that she could not miss that wonderful moment and so she can be there to eat it up. But, she is really the one on a leash, sitting there lonely and waiting for the arrival of the sober caring man who is rarely present. She said, through her tears, "It is worth the wait!" Here, I think she was demonstrating the Kleinian appreciation for the conflict between the death and life instincts. She choked the life out of herself by putting herself on a leash, preventing growth, difference, and change all in the hopes of finding life among the ruins of this broken, dying object.

Sally went on to say she is convinced that moving to Hollywood is the answer to all her problems: socially, financially, and emotionally. She said, "I have realized that all my problems are geographical, not psychological." Here, I again felt discarded, devalued, and forgotten. I wondered why she had to run away from me so violently. So, I interpreted that she was scared to face what was on the inside, what she would find with me. I said her description of the "pain in the ass, depressing, difficult town she lived in and all the distant, shallow people whom she never made friends with" were a reflection of the difficult turmoil she felt inside. So, she was trying to escape the pain and anxiety of dealing with how she felt about herself by turning to the external glamour of Hollywood and the promise of excitement and love she imagined. She was running away from the anxiety of being with me and facing herself. Instead, she was escaping to the immediate fix of the Hollywood phantasy where everyone was famous and happy. Sally replied on a very concrete level, telling me about the better housing prices and better weather.

It is hard to know where this case will go at this point. Sally may indeed quit and move to Hollywood in search of this instant magic. She may stay in treatment and reluctantly work out some of her internal struggles in the same rocky, tug-of-war manner she has already established in the transference, or she may simply end treatment and continue to live the same unhappy life she currently feels trapped in. This is one of the unknown places that the analyst must contend with when working with borderline and narcissistic patients who present with loud, sharp, and scattered transferences highlighted by projective identification dynamics.

As illustrated throughout this chapter, it is best to stay close to the clinical material and the heat of the transference as it unfolds. Valuing the complete nature of countertransference and using it to guide interpretive approaches helps deal with the constant and often invasive quality of projective identification that occurs with such patients. Lack of overall clarity is common when dealing with these loud but scattered transference states.

When anxious, it is easy for the analyst to try and pin things down to genetic reconstruction or to an extra-transference focus. But, we can bring some degree of clinical clarity and gradual insight to the patient if we tolerate not knowing where we are going and instead simply try to understand the immediate, here-and-now situation that is unfolding in the room and within the transference. The immediate clinical moment is often the most complex and confusing yet valuable spot to be in, stay in, and strive to fully understand.

II

A GIFT TO THE ALTER: GENEROSITY, PRIMITIVE GUILT, AND SELF-PROTECTION

Pathological Aspects of Giving and Receiving

Conflicts within the Paranoid/ Depressive Spectrum

The psychoanalytic approach to treatment illustrated in this chapter is based on Melanie Klein's understanding of infantile mental development and the subsequent unconscious struggles with internal conflicts between self and other. Expanding Freud's work through her own study of infants and later adult patients, Klein outlined the natural development of object relations from the earliest days after birth, emphasizing that the ego is object related from the beginning. Klein thought that the innate forces of the life-and-death instinct can promote healthy development and progression of the reality principle or can inhibit and distort these strivings. Love, hate, and the desire for knowledge are the core mental forces that shape all perspective of self and object, and it is within these arenas that growth or pathology emerges.

Klein outlined the predictable conflicts of development as centering upon the paranoid-schizoid position (Klein 1946) with its emphasis on splitting, fears of persecution and annihilation, and the depressive position with its emphasis on fear of harming the object and the desire for reparation. Projective identification is the primary method of managing these internal conflicts. This psychic dynamic can promote and fortify healthy development or retard, destroy, or pathologically speed up the psychological maturational process. The overall rate of and quality of the infant's emotional maturity are influenced by powerful aggressive impulses, constitutional factors, and external life situations. Offsetting these obstacles are the important forces of love, guilt, and creativity. Love and guilt push the ego to find ways of repairing the damage between self and object and creating new and improved object relations. New and better objects are sought out, and healthier solutions to internal conflicts are built. Again, projective identification is the primary vehicle for excessive, perverted, and destructive object relational bonds as well as the path to growth, resolution, and healing.

External interference of this natural growth and balance can come from a lack of good experiences with important objects in the form of parents, siblings, and others, or it can come from the internal operation of excessive envy of and/or aggression toward the good inner object. The earliest anxieties emerge in the paranoid-schizoid position in which the world is predominated with bad persecutory objects as a result of the intense projection of pain and aggression. This is hopefully balanced through splitting, by the wish for union with the all perfect good object. As normal development proceeds, the ego and object become experienced as whole, and the depressive position (Klein 1935, 1940) comes into the forefront. This shift in emotional experience brings on ambivalence, guilt, and fear of loss as a result of hurting or disappointing the object. Forgiveness and reparation bring hope and faith into the infant's view of the world, along with symbolism and creativity.

This chapter explores the idea that for some patients, they are caught within an emotional crossfire of both paranoid and depressive conflicts without any psychic retreat (Steiner 1993) to seek refuge in. The two case examples demonstrate the spectrum of such clinical problems in that the first patient is more firmly grounded in the depressive position but suffers from a core paranoid-schizoid phantasy that shapes all of her depressive ways of organizing life and her relationships to self and other.

The second case demonstrates a patient more rooted in the paranoid-schizoid position, but also maintaining a fragile, immature foothold in the depressive position. Therefore, both patients bring a complicated, mixed bag of phantasies, fears, and psychological struggles to the transference, both dealing with fragmented and perverted visions of what constitutes giving and receiving. In fact, for patients like the two presented in this paper, giving and taking easily become distorted into confusing and conflicting images of control, demand, abandonment, loss, greed, rescue, award, and angry martyrdom.

Melanie Klein and her contemporary followers have built a complex and vital system of psychoanalytic understanding that is directly clinical and always focused on the moment-to-moment interaction of patient and analyst. The interaction of transference, countertransference, projective identification, and the resulting dynamic of interpretation are vital to the successful dynamics of psychoanalytic treatment. In working with patients who are caught in the paranoid/depressive spectrum of conflicts regarding giving and receiving, need and debt, or control and loss, the Kleinian method of moment-to-moment, here-and-now focus on establishing analytic contact (Waska 2007) within the total transference (Joseph 1985) and complete countertransference (Waska 2007) is essential.

CASE MATERIAL

After seeing Sally and Rick for four sessions of couple's therapy, Rick announced he would not return. He was depressed, angry, extremely adversarial, withholding, and unwilling to engage in any sort of dialogue. I was the third therapist he "fired." I suggested Sally continue on her own.

The first time I met with her one-on-one, Sally revealed that Rick was an alcoholic and had been getting drunk almost every day for years. This often caused fights with their teenage daughter and left the family on pins and needles. None of this had come out previously. Also, Sally disclosed how depressed Rick had been, perhaps even suicidal at times, and how hopeless she felt about the marriage. At the same time, Sally felt that if she simply tolerated the situation and tried to be supportive to Rick, he might come around and be a better husband and become happier with his life. I pointed out that this "ignore it and see what happens" strategy hadn't worked yet in the last ten years. Sally agreed but said, "I don't see any other way except to leave him, and how could I do that to the family?"

So, over the next few months, we explored Sally's way of trying to control and manage her husband and her internal objects in an effort to win their love, prevent their collapse and/or enraged revenge, and to prove how loyal and nice she was, denying any ill feelings along the way. I interpreted a pattern of focusing on and controlling the object as a way to avoid being needy or ever having her own desires, which she imagined would hurt and/or enrage the object. In this need-free zone, Sally never had to ask, never had to be disappointed, and never had to face the pain of separation or loss. Control was her link to the object and a way to never face loss, rejection, or guilt.

As I arrived at my office for a session with Sally, I pulled in next to her. We had about five or ten minutes before our appointment. As I got out of my car, she said from her rolled-down window, "Do you need a few minutes? Take your time!" In the countertransference, I felt controlled and wanted to tell her to stop monitoring what I want, mind your own business, and be quiet since we still have five minutes before our session. Reflecting on this feeling, I was then able to make interpretations about her need to control me and make sure I was OK, happy, and not burdened by her. Sally told me she thinks of me as "busy, needing to make phone calls, having to collect myself, deal with paperwork, and generally needing a few minutes to gather myself." I interpreted that she saw me in a weakened state that required her attention, healing, and management. She agreed and said she "had never really thought about it, but now that she is, she thinks she sees most people that way." I commented that if she is surrounded by weakened, burdened people, she is going to feel anxious, guilty, and will want to control and heal us all. She said, she thinks she "spends a lot of time doing that to people, especially my family."

In a recent session, I noticed that she came in and essentially began anxiously reporting her recent "progress" and telling me how she was very uncomfortable with the idea of having to give her husband an ultimatum. After listening to this defensive apology for a bit, I interpreted that she imagined I was demanding that she stage an intervention with her alcoholic husband and either put him into rehab or divorce him. I said it must make her very anxious to feel she would have to do this to please me or get me off her back, when it wasn't what she wanted to do. Sally said, "I do feel you want me to do that and it is scary. I feel if I take any of that kind of action, I will end up hurting somebody. And, I don't want to do that." I interpreted, "So, you feel caught in the middle of either disappointing me and not doing the homework you imagine I am demanding or hurting all these other people who are important to you." She agreed and said she thought I really wanted her to "take action" and was surprised to hear otherwise. I interpreted, "When you try and control others or imagine I am trying to control you, one thing is missing from the picture. You are excluding yourself from everything. When you control us, what you need, what you feel, and how you think are hidden behind trying to please me. I think you are trying to prevent the risk of needing me or wanting my help. By trying to help us all and save us all, you avoid wishing I could help you or save you." Sally looked very surprised. She said, "I never have considered myself to be part of the picture. Never."

In the next session, I found myself ready to demand that Sally kick her husband out of the house if he didn't go to rehab. It's been ten years and nothing has worked, so it's either now or never, I reasoned with myself. I was able to reflect on this countertransference phantasy by nature of it not being my style to begin with and by the sheer intensity of the feeling. I realized it was probably part of a projective identification process from the last session in which I had been partly affected by Sally's own desire to control and fix mixed with her chronic resentment and impatience over her husband's long-standing alcoholism and depression.

So, I used this insight to now interpret that she may be taking my attention to her own needs and desires as a signal to be selfish, forceful, and mean. In other words, to Sally, paying attention to herself and her feelings meant being greedy and demanding. So, to protect her objects, she ignored her own needs. In response, Sally breathed a sigh of relief and said, "I really thought you were going to come down hard on me and say I should take action now. I don't want to do that, I don't want to hurt him, especially when he is so down." I repeated my interpretation, saying, "You are surprised I am thinking of you and your needs, since you never do. But, I think you worry that focusing on your needs means unleashing this demanding, mean person." Sally started to cry and said, "I don't know how to be me, I worry I could be asking for too much."

As we proceeded to talk about her wish to fix her husband and find some way to "make him whole again" and "save him from this terrible place he seems so lost in," I interpreted that she wanted a guarantee of love and attention instead of the terrible place she would feel lost in if she let go and took care of herself. I said she was very much afraid of loss and loneliness, so she kept that away by keeping her finger in the dike no matter what. Sally responded, "I am afraid of letting Rick down, leaving him on his own when he is so unstable and helpless. I don't want to let him down." I interpreted, "You feel that, plus I think you are worried about letting me down, so you must feel trapped in the middle," alluding to her frequent oedipal position of feeling in the middle of two issues or objects and having to find a way to be in charge and control of the outcome at any cost.

Sally told me, "I do feel that way. I always end up feeling like I am in the middle of a mess, trying to sort it out and keep things going." I interpreted, "You say you do that to be good to the other person and please us all. But, I think the bigger reason is you are afraid we won't love you if you stop controlling us. In other words, it looks like you are trying to force others to like you and love you and that you are very afraid that if you let go, we won't care, and you will be all alone." Sally started to cry and nodded yes.

In a recent session, Sally told me she was proud of herself and wanted to share "some examples of finally standing up for myself." She told me of how she had told her husband that she was "really turned off by his rude and self-ish behavior at a family dinner over the weekend." And, she had told him that she was sick of having to cover for his chores when he disappeared for a drink and never comes back to do the laundry or leaves everything in the washing machine. This was indeed a different way for Sally to be relating, actually thinking of how she felt and how he was impacting her.

At the same time, in the countertransference, I felt she was trying to impress me a bit. So, I asked her if she was sharing this victory for her own sake or to make me feel good too. She said, "Well, I felt good for myself, but I also noticed that I was hoping the more I took care of myself, maybe Rick would start to want to take care of himself." I said, "It is very hard for you to not keep an eye on the other person, to make sure we are going to be OK. Without us being happy or well, you are worried where you are?" Here, I introduced the idea that Sally controlled us for her own benefit, not just for the benefit of the object.

Sally said, "I don't know if I could make it own my own. I need him, and he needs me. I know that sounds sick, but I feel like I need to have some kind of backup plan if I need help. I don't think I could take care of myself." With my gentle probing, Sally explained that she not only saw her husband as "on the edge and needing constant care and attention" but herself as constantly on the edge of loneliness and desolation. In fact, I wondered if she used her role of caretaker for him to defend against a much more primitive and hopeless sense of herself, as someone unable to function without the constant attachment of someone, anyone.

So, first I said, "It looks like you are the caretaker and nurse for him and he is nurse and caretaker for you. And, it looks like you are worried that if you don't have him around, you will perish." Sally thought about it for a few minutes and said, "I feel I will probably become frail and demented in so many years. I don't think I will be able to take care of my finances alone. I don't want to give up the comforts I have now and I don't want to face what seems like a nightmare out there in the future. At least I would have someone to watch over me and guide me in the right direction if I wasn't able to take care of myself. I don't know when I will need him that way but I want to be sure I have it figured out now." I said, "It looks like you are already feeling that you hang on by a thin thread and without him you will perish. Without your caretaker, it will be fatal." Sally replied, "Fatal is a good word. That is exactly how it feels. It will be fatal."

DISCUSSION

Sally clung to a sense of desperate hope that seemed to save her from facing the cruel and frightening reality of her fallen object and her own vision of herself without that object. Searles (1977) and Potamianou (1992) point out how manic hope can serve as a shield against harsh reality or the painful acceptance of loss and despair. For Sally, she insisted that if she only tried harder, maybe one day (Akhtar 1996) she could make her object change and transform into a new and healthy object that could take care of himself and take care of her.

Steiner (1984) notes that all defensive aspects of the patient's unconscious conflicts will be relived in the transference. These aspects of the internal world will rise to life through projections of self and object into the analyst alongside certain actions and tone of relating that are meant to recruit us into acting out with them. Sally tried to enlist me into being the cruel, angry, demanding part of herself who wanted to demand an intervention or to leave her husband outright. I followed Joseph's (1983) method of closely monitoring and investigating how my patient tried to use me in her internal struggles. In following this contemporary Kleinian approach and using it to establish and maintain analytic contact (Waska 2007), I was able to interpret her efforts at controlling her objects to save them and her efforts to ultimately try and save herself from a phantasy of desolation, loss, and fatal collapse.

CASE MATERIAL

I have been treating Jack for several years, two to three times a week on the couch. He suffers with great instability about his personal worth to the object and the object's withholding all the love and rewards he needs and feels he deserves. Compared to the last case, Jack is a much rougher mix of paranoid and depressive anxieties and leans much more into the persecutory realm than Sally.

Jack is a high-powered executive who makes a great deal of money and is well known and respected in his field. Inside, however, he felt like a little child who is unloved and always on the verge of being forgotten or punished. He is very sensitive to wanting to give to the underdog, wanting to please the withholding authority, and wanting to be rewarded with greatness for his efforts.

Recently, Jack has been telling me how worried he was that he would not make enough money at his new job to pay the bill. In the same breath, he was subtly dropping stories about painting his yacht over the weekend, how he will make a million in the first year at his new job, and how a movie star is renting his villa in South America. In the countertransference, I found myself feeling envy, spite, and anger. The degree of these feelings helped me to see that Jack wanted to boast in this disguised, secret way but then feeling anxious about my possible reaction. I make that interpretation and Jack agreed. He added, "If I boast, you will put me down and see me as arrogant. But, if I do it secretly, then you might reassure me by saying wait a minute, you have a yacht and know movie stars. You will be OK."

I interpreted that this pull for my love and assurance is temporary since he is always hungry for more and believes what he has is never going to last. Jack associated to how he was so grateful to the new boss who hired him; he wants to send him all sorts of gifts. In the past when this feeling surfaced, we discovered this to be a reverse of the reassurance cycle in which he feels he will now have to constantly thank the other. I make this interpretation, and he says, "Oh, so you have to put me in my place again. Why is it always about something? Why am I always unable to do it right?" I interpret that now I am the disappointing person who doesn't love or understand him. He agrees and says, "Just tell me it is all going to be OK." I say, "Or else I am the bad withholding person. You demand my love, and if I don't give it to you in the perfect way you want, I am not on your side. You are not too flexible or forgiving. Maybe that is exactly what you are afraid of in the world." He said, "I know, I know. But, when is it going to get better???" I said, "It already has, but you are forcing me to be the one that says that, instead of you holding that inside of you so you can use it as a place of security whenever you want." He said, "I like that idea. I want to feel stable all the time without having to constantly question myself every minute of every day like a rabid dog lunging at my throat." This image of himself as the rabid killer dog alternated with the image of me and others hunting him down and always lunging at him for more.

At the start of a recent session, Jack said, "Coming here today I felt so lonely and then I felt better because I knew I was coming to see you and I was looking forward to talking with you. I thought you would be able to help me and show me how to get through these terrible feelings. But, then I realized you would make me look at exactly how I feel and I would have to relive all of it and sit in this shitty pain and I thought to myself, "Fuck Dr. Waska. He can't make me do that! I could be home having a beer, relaxing and watching television, feeling good. Fuck him!"

So, we began the session exploring how in the transference he divides things into me being the good doctor who will show him the way out of pain and me the bad doctor who will force him to live in pain. Jack was unable to integrate these images into a whole object phantasy of having painful feelings and working through them with my help. He wanted me to magically take all bad away and make everything all good.

This splitting problem came up later in the session when he described two situations which he experienced as completely separate and unrelated. He told me of how he saw his neighbor's daughter crying in the yard because her dog had just run away. Jack identified with this child as he described her being "completely lost, broken, and devastated." Jack quickly projected his broken self into the child and "started weeping uncontrollably, praying the parents would find the poor child's pet." He also broke down when they did find the dog, feeling "untold relief and finally able to breathe again." He sobbed as he told me the story as well.

Later in the same session, he told me how he had attended an award ceremony of his coworker's eight-year-old child. Jack said, sobbing, "I had to fight back the tears as I witnessed this completely innocent and pure little child, protected from the world and in a world of her own joy, so cute and so protected." I interpreted, "You want to have that perfect, protected pure state with me and others, but it is so ideal and perfect that of course anything can mess it up and then you feel completely lost and desperate like the little girl with her lost dog." Here, I put together the two aspects of his splitting. I continued, "You have a hard time giving up that wonderful bliss you picture, but always trying to reach that state means you always fall short and feel like a failure."

Jack said, "I know. I really know it is by facing these things that I will find some balance. But, it is so hard to deal with it." I said, "Only if you think you have to do it all alone." So, here was a moment of integration in that instead of how he felt at the beginning of the session, with me being a bad doctor forcing him to feel pain, he realized it was by facing the pain that he could find his way out of it. But, he still had a difficult time imagining that we could do it together. So, he gained a moment into the depressive position, coming up for air out of the clutches of more disturbed paranoid phantasies.

Our schedules usually prevent meeting more often, but we try to when possible. Recently, I offered Jack an extra session at my second office location, about twenty minutes away. He had been there before but usually in the morning. This appointment time was in the late afternoon. When I offered the session to him, I said, "I can see you at that time. There will be traffic at that time of day but I think you should be able to miss the most of it." He said he would be there, but the next day he was about ten minutes late. Jack said as he walked over to the analytic couch, "I guess I didn't miss the traffic!"

I began to reply, "Well, I mentioned that you might—." He interrupted and said, "I had a fair amount of time to look around the roads and notice all the work they are doing. I can be a bit of a traffic geek. I like to see what new projects are going on. From the looks of it, the new work will make things move much faster in both directions. Coming from the other direction a few times on the weekend, I got stuck pretty badly. I think the work will eliminate that. Well, I have something about work to bring up, but I am not looking forward to it. I don't want to see your reaction. I am certainly not happy with it myself."

Now, two issues were occurring that I was not aware of until later in the session and even until later that week. But, upon reflection of my countertransference feelings and my general interpretive stance, I believe I missed out on two matters. First of all, when I started to say, "Well, I mentioned that you might—," I was both reminding him that we had talked about the chance of traffic and then I was going to say we should think of other better times in the future. So, I think I was initially defensive and then was going to be somewhat apologetic. In other words, I was somewhat responding in the countertransference to his sarcastic remark of "Well, I guess I didn't miss the traffic." I acted out instead of interpreting his frustration or anger with me. The second matter was my missing out on the displaced references to the transference. When Jack talked about how all the work on the freeway was going to make things so much better, he was talking about how things were not very good now. Also, when he said he used to get stuck in the traffic on weekends, I think this was a disguised reference to him being angry at being stuck in traffic today.

Jack continued, saying, "I feel very embarrassed about how I reacted at work. You know we have been exploring how I feel so rejected and forgotten by them and how I try so hard to not let that leak out. It keeps happening." Here, I again had a chance to address the transference, but I was lost in the displacement to work. We can never be on top of every clinical moment, but it is also useful to try and understand how and why we were not able to think analytically in those particular moments. And, it is rare that we have only one chance to explore things. Most of the time, we can bring up the issue at another time and find other places where the interpretation works just as well. However, whether it is in the moment or later, the mutative power of the interpretation has to do with its link to the immediate transference and the current unconscious phantasy state.

So, Jack told me about how he "had reacted so poorly at work again. You know we have been talking about how I feel so rejected and forgotten by them and how I try so hard to not let that leak out, to not end up acting pathetic or angry, but it keeps happening. During a conference call, I said I thought things could be brought back from the dead to the land of the living by focusing more on our goals, and then I had a few specific recommendations. Now, I am the new kid on the block at the firm, but I thought I was really trying hard to find some solutions for the team. Well, I am frustrated and embarrassed to tell you this because it seems I am always putting my foot in my mouth and everyone sees what is really going on underneath the surface." I said, "You are worried I am upset with you for not growing up and flying right and I might be fed up with you messing up instead." He said, "Yes. I want to make you happy but I am sure I end up pissing you off and everyone else off. Maybe you will just give up on me, tired of beating a dead horse." Jack continued, "So, one of my managers, the one on the team that I was making the 'bring it back from the dead' comments about, said I was being 'flippant.' I was shocked. It was my worst nightmare. Now, I have a reputation as the flippant guy!"

I said, "Maybe you are anxious to say it more straightforwardly and risk the consequences. So, you disguise it with sarcasm." He added, "Or humor." I associated in my mind to when he arrived at the session and I was now able to gain some clarity about what may have been occurring in the transference and my countertransference denial and acting out. So, I said, "You walked in and said something to me about the traffic that was sort of flippant. Maybe, because you felt anxious being honest with me about how you felt with the traffic you were flippant instead. You don't want a conflict with me but you are somewhat aggressive by being flippant so it could actually create a feeling of conflict." Here, I was interpreting the projective identification component of his actions, internally and interpersonally.

Jack replied, "Oh shit. I am busted. I tried to not say anything negative and thought I could just be cute instead. The minute you started to say something in response, I thought you were going to say, 'I TOLD YOU THERE WOULD BE TRAFFIC, SO WHY ARE YOU COMPLAINING?'" Here, I realized that Jack was responding to something that in fact was occurring. Through his flippant remark, he had managed to nudge me in the direction of feeling a minor sense of irritation and parental judgment, hence my somewhat parental message of "Well, I did mention the possibility of—" in response to what I must have felt to be challenging and judgmental from him. Betty Joseph (1985) and other modern Kleinians have noted that patients find unconscious ways of inviting us to join them in their internal struggles by acting out within the clinical transference and countertransference interaction. So, there was something real about what he worried about in the transference, but he also quickly amplified it and imagined it to be something to quickly control, defuse, and eliminate.

Jack continued, "So, I tried to cut you off before you could take me to task. I wanted to smooth it out as soon as possible." I interpreted the projective identification process by saying, "I actually was starting to say that I had mentioned the possible traffic, so it looks like you did encounter it and we should plan for that in the future and find better times. At the same time, I can see how you may have felt I was starting to sound parental or irritated. But, I think you quickly coated me with additional anger and quickly put yourself under my thumb so then you had to quickly find a way to make the peace between us." He added, "And, when you say that this time might not be good so we should plan for that in the future, I want to immediately say that the whole idea of coming to this office is not good because otherwise you might suggest another time to come here and I would be trapped and have to go along with it or find a way out and escape."

I replied, "So, suddenly it is a power struggle and you will head me off at the pass." He said, "Yes. I am pretty good at making people do my bidding without their ever knowing. I smile them into doing it my way." I replied, "Maybe you do that because you are scared if we were up front and honest with each other, it would get ugly." Jack said, "I am very afraid of that."

He told me he had an experience with his mentor/boss recently that made him feel humiliated and very disappointed with himself. He is currently being trained by this boss who is considered a guru in the business and is very much Jack's hero. So, they go to various clients as a team while Jack is being trained. After the last meeting with the client, the boss took Jack aside and gave him some feedback on the pros and cons of his approach and how to better negotiate with the client in the future. Jack told me he was mortified and felt he had "really screwed up." I interpreted that Jack only wanted praise from his analyst and his boss and anything else felt like terrible criticism or judgmental control. I said he divides what I say into either reassuring praise and comfort or devastating criticism. So, I was focusing on how he shifted us in the transference and in the extra-transference, into wild success or absolute failure, either close and warm or cold and apart.

Jack told me he wanted to share a recent cartoon he saw that "was incredibly funny, just really funny." He said it was a single picture of little Piglet and Winnie-the-Pooh walking along a forest path. Now, in 2009, the global context of this cartoon was that there was a potential swine flu pandemic. Before Jack described the cartoon and the punch line, he was overtaken with laughter about it. That was what I became focused on and caught up in. He laughed very hard about it, and my feeling was that it was strange and slightly frightening how much he suddenly was so taken by this cartoon and how much he seemed to be personally enthralled by it. He told me that little Piglet was thinking to himself that he felt grateful they were the best of friends and so close over the years. And Winnie-the-Pooh was thinking to himself, "If that pig sneezes on me, I will kill him." We were out of time and I thought the cartoon was funny, but I was at a loss of what to say about it.

It was only later that day when I reflected on the situation did I realize more. I could see that this cartoon was part of the total transference (Joseph 1985) situation and it represented his immediate phantasy about his objects and about our relationship. At first, I felt badly about myself that I didn't see such "an obvious transference remark" and felt I was "a loser analyst for not interpreting it right in the moment with clarity and expertise." After a bit, I noticed myself bashing myself in this way and reflected on this countertransference reaction. I came to understand that I was now feeling just as Jack does, either I had to be a perfect, always-on-the-target analyst or I must be a failing and shameful figure. This realization allowed me to forgive myself and give myself permission to make the interpretation sometime in the future when it seemed right. It didn't have to be an all-or-nothing circumstance.

So, in the next session, there was an opportunity. Jack was telling me how he wants to not feel so vulnerable and scared of what others think and not have to be so dependent on others for his self-worth. I told him, "You usually look to me for reassurance and warm protection. But, you quickly add so much judgment and demand to it that it becomes a volatile trust that can switch very quickly to something more ominous. I think you really identified with the cartoon last time because you are Piglet wanting closeness and the deep affection and trust but then you get scared and very judgmental of it and put lots of conditions and ramifications on it like Winnie did." Jack replied, "I usually am worried you are Winnie and I am Piglet. I hope you don't want to kill me if I screw up." I added, "But, you also can have the very narrow demanding and fickle approach Winnie has." Jack agreed and said, "That cartoon pretty much sums up how I feel at work all the time." I added, "And everywhere else."

Jack then went on to talk about "his struggles over the weekend, driving to a party through all these rich neighborhoods where people he knows in business circles live, all in houses he can't afford, and they drive cars that put his to shame." He told me how "awash he was with this sense of deprivation and unfairness, like they are the great ones and I am nothing." But, he also reported, "Some progress. I was more aware of seeing everything like that than I ever did before. And, by seeing it more clearly, I did not feel so angry and lonely. When we attended the party in one of those fancy homes, I realized I was sizing up everyone in the room and finding something to cut them down to size about. Yes, he has a $200,000 car, but his wife is fat. Yes, he has sailed around the world and is a famous CEO, but he is probably a horrible parent. But, I noticed myself doing this so I could start to bring myself back to earth and reassure myself a bit."

I said, "So, you could remember that you matter to and didn't have to attack others to save yourself." Jack said, "Yes. And, that is a great deal of progress, and I think we have come a long way. But, at the same time, I am lying here thinking to myself that if I keep telling you these wonderful tales of success, I will impress you, and one day you will say you are very proud of me, and I can finally graduate and leave therapy. So, I am trying to please you and get you to give me a get out of jail card. Shit! Why am I still doing that? And, at the same time, I feel like I hate the fact that I need to impress you and that I need you in any shape or form. I want to scream out to him that I don't need him to make progress. I can do it on my own. Fuck him! I am doing it my way, not his way!"

I interpreted, "It sounds like one minute you are Piglet and the next minute you are Winnie. It is very difficult for you to trust me, lean on me, and show me all these painful struggles without it turning into somebody rejecting somebody, some kind of anger and hurt." Jack nodded and shed a few tears.

DISCUSSION

Jack was struggling under the constant depressive fear of losing the object's love and being abandoned. But, because of his more borderline and narcissistic propensity to envy, greed, and the impatient desire for an ideal union with an ideal object, this state of mind was easily and frequently tipped over into a much more paranoid-schizoid experience in which his ideal self became worthless and the loving arms of his desired ideal object turned into the tentacles of an attacking and rejecting bad object.

Klein (1957) elaborated the differences between envy, greed, and jealousy. Many of the patients, who, like Jack, have a very precarious hold in the depressive position, seem to have a perverse preoccupation with all three feelings and experience crippling and primitive phantasies that are fused with all three elements. Spillius (1993) has noted that as the individual reaches the depressive position, he or she becomes much more in touch with the fact that the object is not only needed and necessary, but that the object has its own separate existence, identity, and relationship with other objects. This realization stirs up even more envy, greed, and jealousy, and for some patients such as Jack, this creates a retreat back into or a collapse back into more paranoid-schizoid functioning. When Jack noticed differences between himself and others or noted the separation between himself and others through money, ability, position, appearance, possessions, or other external methods of tally, envy came into play as an extension of the death instinct to destroy evidence of difference and separation.

In the transference, Jack used projective identification to convey these states of primitive rage, loss, envy, and oral demand. I was to be the loyal aid who would always reassure him. If I did not, I was the cruel judge and rejecter. This was the mix of communication, attack, and expelling that

Rosenfeld (1983) spoke of. Jack felt the need for a container that would accept his depressive longing, guilt, and desire to please. But, because he was so aggressive with his demand for immediate love, reassurance, and perfection, he unconsciously felt this container was either unable to tolerate his desires or unwilling to hold his anxiety and confusion for very long without rejecting it and circling back to punish him for daring to thrust such contamination into the object. So, the ideal object was overly desired and then feared and seen as unsafe and withholding. This nightmare version of give and take came alive in the transference as well.

The Kleinian approach and my own Kleinian method of establishing analytic contact are designed to find out how the patient's mind works and gradually convey that knowledge to the patient through interpretation and putting words to the nature of the transference. This process can become bogged down or derailed by the patient's efforts at turning away from their core anxieties and instead seeking to maintain their current pathological psychic equilibrium and avoid change, growth, or differentiation. This often takes the form of intense projective identification efforts that can either draw the analyst into various enactments and overinvolvements (Schoenhals 1996) or acting out in a rejecting and stoic manner, as the pathologically distant observer.

Not all patients suffering from depressive anxieties present the same type of transference problems. Indeed, there are a number of patients, illustrated in this chapter with case material, who are trapped in very intense and primitive aspects of the depressive position in which there are often aspects of the paranoid-schizoid position present as well. So, phantasies of persecution and feelings of envy can be present. Devaluation and idealization can occur. And, the anxieties regarding loss, guilt, and punishment can be overwhelming and without any hope of restitution, resurrection, or integration.

Therefore, the need for consistent, focused work within the transference, countertransference, and projective identification matrix is very important. These premature depressive states or extremely fragile and unstable depressive methods of relating frequently shift into more outright paranoid feelings and persecutory phantasies that bring the normally more reliable depressive position into a much more precarious state of experience. For these very troubled patients, the healthy aspects of giving and receiving are corrupted into frightening, desperate, and angry cycles of demand, betrayal, attack, and endless loss.

4

Varieties of Depressive Anxiety

Fragile Patients in the Fray

Melanie Klein's entire theoretical stance broadly expanded Isaacs's (1948) ideas of phantasy as a mental representation of the instincts, focusing on the manner in which the mind seeks out the illusion of gratification and omnipotent fulfillment. Hanna Segal (1977) has extended Klein's views and describes how splitting, projection, and introjections are the leading mechanisms in phantasy, and in favorable development, the ego becomes stronger through introjection and identification with the good ideal object, and violent projection is much less needed, providing room for integration and reality testing. Interference with this hopeful outcome can come from internal or external factors. I would add that it is often a vicious cycle between both.

Melanie Klein outlined the predictable conflicts of development as centering upon the paranoid-schizoid position (Klein 1946) with its emphasis on splitting, fears of persecution and annihilation, and the depressive position with its emphasis on fear of harming the object and the desire for reparation. Projective identification is the primary method of managing these internal conflicts, and the mode of use can promote and fortify healthy development or retard, destroy, or pathologically speed up the psychological maturational process. Love, guilt, and creativity push the ego to find ways of repairing the damage between self and object and creating new and improved object relations. New and better objects are sought out, and healthier solutions to internal conflicts are built. Again, projective identification is the primary vehicle for excessive, perverted, and destructive object relational bonds as well as the path to growth, resolution, and healing.

Strachey (1934) investigated how and when an interpretation is therapeutic, and he postulated that an interpretation advances change when it is focused on the moment of urgency in the transference. It is a verbalization of the immediate emotional transference state. Melanie Klein has pioneered the current view in psychoanalysis that interpretation should be about the interaction of the patient and analyst at an intra-psychic level (O'Shaugnessy 1983). Klein advocated a technique of interpreting both positive and negative object relations in the transference from the first moment of treatment to the final days of termination. The Kleinian approach has discovered the importance of tracking the patient's primitive defenses and mode of nonverbal communication. This is often through the vehicle of projective identification, in which anxiety, anger, desire, and curiosity are transmitted in a subtle or at other times quite forceful manner. Klein discovered projective identification to be the infant's first way of communicating with its object. Bion (1962a, 1962b) extended her ideas and found that projective identification was the primary vehicle for both defense and communication. Rosenfeld (1988) has elaborated on the different types of projective identification and the different motives for utilizing it. These include communication, expelling/attacking, or both. Steiner (1989) points out that evacuation and efforts at linking with the object often occur together in complex efforts to invite the analyst to contain, learn, and translate the unbearable feelings and thoughts the patient is experiencing.

In broadening Klein's work to match today's clinical climate, I have developed (Waska 2005, 2006, 2007) the use of Kleinian technique in all aspects of clinical practice, with all patients, in all settings. Regardless of frequency, use of couch, length of treatment, or style of termination, the goal of psychoanalytic treatment is always the same: the understanding of unconscious phantasy, the resolution of intra-psychic conflict, and the integration of self/object relations, both internally and externally. The psychoanalyst uses interpretation as their principal tool, with transference, countertransference, and projective identification being the three clinical guideposts of those interpretive efforts.

By attending to the interpersonal, transactional, and intra-psychic levels of transference and phantasy with consistent here-and-now and in-the-moment interpretation, the Kleinian method can be therapeutically successful with neurotic, borderline, narcissistic, or psychotic patients, whether being seen as individuals, couples, or families and at varied frequencies and duration.

The Kleinian method of Analytic Contact strives to illuminate the patient's unconscious object relational world, gradually providing the patient a way to understand, express, translate, and master their previously unbearable thoughts and feelings. We make analytic contact with their deepest experiences so they can make personal and lasting contact with their full potential.

Successful analytic contact involves not only psychic change, but a corresponding sense of loss and mourning. So, every moment analytic contact is both an experience of hope and transformation as well as dread and despair as the patient struggles with change and a new way of being with himself and others. Successful analytic work always results in a cycle of fearful risk taking, hasty retreats, retaliatory attacks, anxious detours, and attempts to shift the treatment into something less than analytic, something less painful. The analyst interprets these reactions to the precarious journey of growth as a way of steering the treatment back to something more analytic, something that contains more meaningful contact with self and other. The support that we give our patients includes the inherent vow that we will help them survive this painful contact and walk with them into the unknown.

DEPRESSIVE ISSUES AND THE TRAUMA OF SEPARATION/INDIVIDUATION

Espasa (2002) considers Klein's notion of the depressive position (Klein 1935, 1940) from two places. The first is the onset of depressive phantasies of terrible death and/or destruction to the object, followed hopefully by the more mature, integrated phase of depressive phantasies regarding restoration, repair, and forgiveness. Steiner (1992) also notes the more difficult phase of depressive loss in which the loss is denied and even attacked as something threatening and dangerous. Here, Grotstein's (2000) ideas of the defensive and protective aspects of the death instinct come into play. Grinberg (1964) has termed this attacking guilt "persecutory guilt," a phase in which the aggression toward the object is turned inwards to protect the object. I would add and emphasize the motive to protect the self from the possible retaliation of the object.

Here, it is as if the object has been killed off and annihilated but now then returns from the grave for revenge. This awful phantasy eclipses hope for understanding, negotiation, forgiveness, reconsideration, reversal, or repair. Bicudo (1964) notes that some patients are barely able to reach the depressive position in their psychological development and therefore still rely heavily on the use of splitting and projective identification to deal with intense guilt feelings. They view the object as either forcing them to feel badly about their desires and autonomy or forcing them to give credit to their objects for any self-defining action.

I would add that idealization is one dynamic patients use to deal with this persecutory guilt but that defense sets up a brittle situation destined to fail, collapse, and disappoint. Grotstein (2005) noted that there is often an unconscious recruitment of the analyst, via projective identification, to become an idealized maternal figure who comes to the rescue of the lost, forgotten child. In this phantasy, the patient is reluctant to accept becoming mature, separate, independent, and able to define their own world because of the dread of obligation, guilt, and persecutory suffering. So, if the patient feels the analyst refuses this role, they become angry, betrayed, fearful, and confused.

CASE MATERIAL

John had seen me for two years before he stopped attending and didn't return my calls. He had originally started coming to treatment because he "knew he better get his shit together and maybe lay off some of the drugs." He has returned to see me four months ago and told me that "after sinking to a new low with the narcotics," he went to a detox program and has not used opiates or cocaine since. John realizes the other drugs he takes and the excessive drinking are not helpful to his overall well-being, but he says, "It is all a work in progress, Doc." We now meet on a regular basis, and John remains motivated and committed like before, but this loyalty is of course colored and distorted by his transference phantasies.

When he first started seeing me, John was twenty-two at the time, working as a shipyard mechanic. He was having troubles with his girlfriend, who disapproved of his daily pot smoking and "would have thrown him out on his ass if she knew about all the narcotics, the coke, and the fall-down drinking." Over the course of two years, we examined the ways John was very submissive to her and others, always trying to please everyone and avoid conflict. This was part of an enormous sense of anxiety he lived with. While John avoided telling his girlfriend the truth and acted like a shipyard mechanic with most of his friends, he also showed a much more vulnerable side when he said he was "very frustrated that she didn't want to talk about her feelings and have an emotional dialogue. She is a freaking clam!" The more John tried to hide his drug use from her and his guilt around it, the more distant he felt from her. At the same time, possibly for reasons of her own, she pulled away from him, and eventually he found out that she was seeing someone else. They broke up, and he struggled to meet other women. This brought out the incredible level of fear and anxiety he lived within. His girlfriend provided a stable and safe emotional island, but now John felt completely alone and like a small child lost in a world of angry, demanding, fragile, and volatile adults whom he has to please by following their footsteps or risk being punished and abandoned.

John was able to feel comfortable, temporarily, by defensively identifying with his highly aggressive father who had plenty of advice on how to dominate women and "how to pull the panties off." So, John would tell me stories of the various women he met up with and his efforts at "pulling those panties off." But, most of these sexual adventures quickly turned into disappointments, and he felt hurt and betrayed. I interpreted that he wanted something more out of the relationship, possibly love and commitment. John agreed some of the time and was able to look at how anxious he was around women. He was uncertain how to talk with them, how to relate to them, and was convinced he would be rejected if he really shared himself with them. So, I interpreted that he used the "pulling the panties off" approach as a tough guy defense to ward off these fears of rejection should he try and get close and reveal his true self to someone.

Here, we began to explore the more passive pleasing approach he used to try and control and win over the object. He had many friends, but they were all drug addicts and alcoholics. So, even with his boss and coworkers, he was quick to agree with their opinions, offer them rides, and buy all their drinks at the bar after work. With his friends, he said he "was sick of all the leeches, but that's all I got." He provided transportation, drugs, concert tickets, and gave them money. But, the more we worked together, the more he was able to tolerate, manage, and work through the anxiety of letting them go and seeking out friends who would respect him and be more of an equal. This last piece was very difficult for John. He wanted to be an equal but also preferred to be less than equal as it gave him a sense of control, lack of conflict, and a way to foster attention.

Indeed, I also interpreted that he used this approach with me in the transference. With me, John was usually awkward, anxious, and polite. He attended religiously, like he had been assigned to see me and needed to fill the obligation. I made that interpretation and he said, "I want to make sure we are OK, I don't need you against me. I am trying to do whatever you see fit!" Here, in the countertransference, I felt quite restricted to the roles he was assigning me. I could only be the commander who tells him what to do or I would be against him. I was aware of the very rigid way he was controlling me and making us into a two-dimensional pair without any choice or independent style of thinking.

I commented about how this pleasing effort left us in a particular leader/follower role which may feel comfortable but also restrictive and with him always having to think of my needs first. He was quite interested in this idea. We had visited this before in the form of him trying to not smoke pot for me, but never really addressing why he was smoking it and if he really wanted to stop. So, there was an ongoing invitation in the countertransference for me to be the guiding parent who would tell him to stop using drugs and get on the straight and narrow, but this was also a way he was inviting me to be the one with autonomous function and him being the neutral empty vessel that would echo my thoughts, feelings, and needs.

During the first two years with John and during the following period of treatment that we are in now, he smoked pot every day, so he was often scattered and nervous when I saw him. During the course of the first two years, he did reduce his drinking and drug use a few times, but never stopped the pot. We established that it was his escape from the mixture of depressive and paranoid (Klein 1946) anxieties that ruled his life. He was using drugs to escape phantasies of being rejected, betrayed, and hurt. He was also using drugs to cope with an intense sense of guilt and fear over being himself and asking others for love rather than feeling he was obligated to serve, hoping for some crumbs of love in return. Of course, I recommended he stop using and drinking, attend 12-step meetings, and consider another rehab program, but he would have nothing to do with it in that concrete way. However, in his own private and somewhat secretive manner, he gradually stopped using most of the drugs and limited himself to certain drugs on special occasions and mostly stuck with smoking pot and having an occasional beer. So, in this way, he was starting to be separate and have his own ideas and pursue them, but created many transference situations that pulled for me to step in and take over that function for him. I found it crucial to interpret this as often as possible.

In the transference, I also felt that John saw me as a surrogate parent, an alternate to his real father and mother. He seemed to need me to be a third alternative to his mother and father's typical way of parenting. In the countertransference, the parallel to this was that I had phantasies of adopting John and raising him in a "normal" environment, safe from the terrible family he was used to. As I examined these feelings of me becoming the ideal father/mother for him, I noticed how this was very complicated. On one hand, it seemed so nice. I would rescue him from his terrible parents, in particular his awful father. Then, we would have this ideal father/son relationship in which I could transmit the good ways of living and have picture-perfect father/son moments where I would share with him the "normal" and healthy ways of life.

On the other hand, this meant I was suddenly controlling his life and molding him into my version of what was right. I was judging his father to be bad and myself to be good and right. This countertransference insight was critical and showed me how to navigate through some of John's more difficult projective identification maneuvers. Indeed, this principle holds for all treatments but was especially moving in John's work. Over the course of the almost three years I have seen him, John's recounting of his father's behavior when he was growing up and his stories of his father's current behaviors made for an easy person to hate. It was no problem for me to picture this man as a very ugly, abusive person who had no clue on how to care for his son. So, the pull was for me to tell John to dump his father, sever the relationship, and find someone better such as myself in the new ideal father role. But, I am very glad I was able to contain, explore, and gradually understand and interpret these dynamics because over the course of time, John's own feelings about his father changed. More and more, he felt less intimidated by him and less angry with him. Bit by bit, he began to initiate more contact with him and revealed his desire to build a better bond with him.

John told me he "felt sorry for the old guy. He is a prick, but he can be a decent prick some of the time." As the months went by, I heard more about John "hanging out with the old fart, kicking it, and having a decent time." At one point, John was visibly touched when he realized how after he told his father he was going camping and timidly asked to borrow some equipment, "out of the blue, he told me he had bought me a hammock so I could chill out in the trees or have a place to take the ladies." This was a new way for them to be together, a way in which there was a shared feeling of enjoying each other's company and respecting each other. There was a new love that was being permitted growth. This was what John wanted. This was his own separate, individual desire. It was different than the anger, hurt, and repulsion he had repeatedly projected into me.

So, if I had insisted that he see his father as I did and write him off as a person he wanted to get close to, I would have been demanding that he bend to my personal opinion and deny any of his own personal hopes or wishes. As it was, by containing and analyzing my countertransference phantasies and feelings in this realm, I allowed John to have his own separate and autonomous mental space to decide how he felt and what he wanted.

As it turned out, his choice was not to write his father off, but rather to slowly develop a new, healthier relationship in which he actually developed boundaries and saw himself as more of an equal man or a deserving son, instead of an inferior bad son. As mentioned, this is an overall principle that is important in all our treatments. If we stop ourselves from becoming the judge and jury of how good or bad our patient's objects are, then we allow them the opportunity, many times for the first time in their lives, to slowly decide exactly how they want not only to see themselves but also how they want to perceive their objects and how to begin relating to those objects within that new phantasy state both internally and externally.

Now, this is often difficult in the countertransference because of subtle or blatant material from the patient that influences how we think and feel about their objects. From John's description, his parents were caring but also very brutal and unable to communicate or foster an atmosphere of emotional sharing and support. John's father used violence and verbal intimidation to rule the house, and both John's parents were extremely aggressive in how they related or non-related as it were. When John described his interactions with his parents, I pictured two motorcycle gang members raising an infant. His father told him, "Fuck the whores and then move on. They are simply places to park your dick when you are not at work." His mother told him, "Be careful of the broads who blow you at the bar. Go for the ones that wait till you get home to swallow." So, in a very crude and disturbing manner, both parents seemed to care for John and his well-being, but their aggressive, dominating, and extreme way of doing so was traumatic for John. Together with their put-downs and his father's violent temper and physical abuse, John ended up feeling very misunderstood, intimidated, and rarely supported. His father was an alcoholic who encouraged John to get drunk with him, even when John told him he was trying to stay sober. John told me, "I was punched so many times growing up, I don't care if he beats me. But, when I hang out with him now and try and have a good time, what really gets to me is how he embarrasses me in public and how he just won't drop that bullshit act when we are just hanging out. I just wish he would act normal."

Here, this was part of the transference in which John wanted me to be the "normal" father who told him what to do, showed him how to live life, and didn't put up a wall of "bullshit" when we were together. As mentioned, I interpreted that he was enlisting me to be a kinder, gentler version of his father but he was inviting me to be just as controlling, judgmental, and intimidating. As a result, John looked to me for guidance, but was very anxious about my expectations of him and my possible disappointment in his actions.

An example of this is how John tried his best to always be on time. During the first few months of our second period of treatment, he was living two hours away. He would drive down in his truck, after smoking some pot and having breakfast, and go back to sleep in his truck, waiting in my parking lot for our morning appointment so as to never be late.

Interpersonally, he was always very anxious about how to relate to me in the moment. When he ran out of whatever he was telling me, he would freeze and look at me with fear. I asked him what was going on and John told me, "I am sure you are thinking how that lame ass should have something else to say." I interpreted that he was making me into a demanding father and then he was trying to find a way to please me. I also said he must be scared that I would not accept him simply being himself, pausing and taking his time in talking to me about whatever might emerge in his thoughts and feelings. John said, "That would be a whole new way of going about things!" Here, we were starting to enter into the realm of two persons able to exist together even if both parties had independent thought and difference. There could be acceptance and understanding and tolerance. But, this was still a very precarious commodity.

The pressure John feels to please, fulfill, and provide what he thinks the object needs, desires, or demands is one of the hallmarks for patients struggling with more primitive depressive phantasies. An example of how this was a constant specter in the transference was when John would talk about some topic and then finish with a moment of uncomfortable silence and sweat on his brow. He would say, "That is it. I am sorry, but that is it. That is all I have got." He was obviously under enormous internal pressure to keep feeding me, keep pleasing me, and keep any conflict at bay. I interpreted how he turned me into a demanding object that must be fed at all times, or else. At other times, in similar circumstances, I have interpreted his internal pressure to please me and keep me close, trying hard to maintain what he feels to be a fragile and conditional love. So, I interpret the two sides of this primitive depressive struggle in which John alternates between feeling he will lose my love completely or he will fail to please me, thereby turning me into an angry, threatening object. It is this dual dilemma that haunts patients such as John, trying to find safety in this unstable, slippery version of the depressive position where separation and individuation can bring on disaster.

In many cases, the phantasy is that separation and difference bring on paranoid-schizoid fears of persecution while individuation brings on depressive fears of abandonment, guilt, rejection, and eternal loneliness.

Over time, I have interpreted these transference phantasies as also creating his anxiety in dating and at the core of his chronic drug and alcohol problems. Coming to me as a son comes to a father for advice on dating, John explained how when he gets a girl's phone number, he "feels excited but really nervous." When he decides it is the right time to call her for the first time, John feels "panic and confusion." His going to his parents for advice on this seemed to add to his own confusion. His father tells him, "Wait three days so she doesn't think you are a whipped pussy. Then, call her and take her out and get those fucking panties off!" John's mother would tell him, "This is a very delicate situation. You have to wait two days to three so you don't look too desperate. But, don't wait more than four or five days because you will look like an inconsiderate jerk. But, don't sound too needy either."

While some of what his parents said was clearly an effort at giving him loving guidance, John was left feeling extremely anxious and sure he could "screw it up twenty ways to Sunday." He told me that prior to calling the girl, he would methodically write out what he was going to say so he could "follow the script without losing my brain and sounding stupid." I interpreted that this was one of many ways he was trying to control what he saw as a very fickle and unstable object. He had to find the right formula to handle it just so to prevent some kind of meltdown. But, I interpreted, this goal of always having to find the correct way to make the object accept him and not be unhappy or angry made him feel constantly on the spot and vulnerable to a very scary object that he wanted to get close to but ended up dreading. I also interpreted that his scripted approach with women was similar to his attempts at finding the right thing to talk about with me and hoping he doesn't run out of topics in the spotlight. Finally, I interpreted that I thought his greatest anxiety came from separating himself from me or the girls, being different from what he perceived our needs to be.

Once separate in his mind, he was scared of whether I was hurt, injured, or angry. Hurting the object or being hurt by the object were now both in play as possible consequences of not being the constantly pleasing loyal servant. Since this was such a place of anxiety, it was difficult to even find the place to bring up the other side of this struggle, but I felt it was crucial to bring up just as often. Once separate from the object, if John felt he and the object had survived, he was now facing being his own individual, unique self. Individuation was upon him, and the experience of having a self that he could define and count on was suddenly before him. I interpreted that this was very scary and he felt desolate and empty, unsure how to build a self and unclear how to be if he stepped away from being on guard for. While this was an emotional integration that was certainly not near, I felt it was important to always bring into focus because otherwise we could become defensively lost in exploring the troubles he had simply separating from the object. These two conflicts are at the heart of patients like John, who struggle with these primitive conflicts which are depressive, but in a very fragile and intense manner that can easily subsume very dangerous paranoid elements as well.

John was very anxious when he stopped trying to please me and was left with himself and what he felt or thought. This felt dangerous, unknown, empty, and confusing. So, it was a real step forward when he reported meeting a girl whom he was sure just "wanted him for his drug connections" and then when told her he had no drugs, instead of being rejected as he anticipated, they spent the day going to lunch and a movie. He reported having "a great time. It was totally unexpected, but lots of fun." It was new for John to picture himself having something to offer from the inside rather than having to please the object with something on the outside.

Over time, we worked on how he applied great pressure to himself to adapt, compromise, and submit to the object, coming into line with whatever was being said or done. I interpreted his fear of being different instead of similar. We worked on this core anxiety of differentiation and the emptiness he experienced when separate and individuated.

John had lived at home his whole life, up to this last year. He was now thirty years old. He had taken comfort living in the basement of his mother's home, since his parents had divorced when he was eight. But, he also felt stifled, trapped, and lonely as he sat by himself, smoking pot and watching television. Since I began seeing him this second period of treatment, he had been caretaking a friend's remote property in the hills several hours from the city. There were acres of trees, no neighbors for miles, and not much of a town to go to except a local general store and a gas station. At first, John felt lonely and unsure how to spend his time. But, over the months and with us discussing it, he grew into this new independence.

For me, it was like watching a teenager go off to camp for the first time. John spoke of the fun of waking up when he wanted to instead of on his mother's schedule. He clearly shared his proud feelings when telling me how he had never cooked for himself before but now he "was cooking up a storm. I am making burgers, hotdogs, enchiladas, and chili. For dessert I am having pie, cake, cupcakes, and ice cream. I love it! I haven't eaten this good ever!"

On one hand, it felt like listening to a teenager gone wild, eating all his favorite foods without any thought of salads or vegetables. I noticed this countertransference nudge to be parental and suggest some broccoli or pasta. On the other hand, I realized he was in fact testing me to see if I would understand his new efforts at "doing his own thing." I said, "You are really proud of what you can do in the kitchen. It sounds like you want me to see how independent and adult you can be on your own, just doing your own thing." John replied, "Damn right! It feels good."

In working with John, I believe I am helping him manage and change some very fundamental and primitive depressive phantasies that a fair number of patients bring to us. There is a core fear of separation due to phantasies of hurting or being hurt and a fear of the nothingness that individuation would bring. Grotstein (1980a) has noted how Betty Joseph emphasizes "establishing contact" with the infantile aspects of the patient. In my own work, I extend this concept to be the overall goal of all analytic work, to establish "analytic contact" (Waska 2007, 2010a, 2010b). The analyst works to make contact with the patient's core unconscious phantasies and object relational conflicts through the use of transference, countertransference, interpretation, and the moment-to-moment exploration of the dynamics of projective identification. While the ego always strives to maintain connection to the nourishing good object, the very act of growth, separation, and individuation is experienced as severing that connection. So, there is an ongoing struggle to assert and to merge, to divide and to blend.

Grotstein (1980b) has discussed how in the depressive position, the subject has to surrender control over the object, withdrawing sadistic attacks and submissive loyalty and making reparation instead. This creates a state of separation and gradual individuation, coupled with the search for a way to maintain connection with the object. In making this depressive parting of the ways, many intense conflicts come into play, the more troubling being the sense of grief and irresolvable loss. Hurting is linked to being hurt, and separation is seen as desolate isolation. Both self and object can become lost forever, irretrievably disconnected and fragmented. The hopeful and healthy alternative is some sense of integration and mutually beneficial separation, leading to a belief in individuation as a safe place to create, grow, and discover rather than a traitorous pit of abandonment and revenge from both sides.

Projective identification is a vital ingredient to development and growth. It provides the symbiotic union as well as primitive separation with the object so vital in the infantile journey through normal paranoid-schizoid transformation. However, Bell (1992) notes that projections, especially the more aggressive, envious, or greedy ones, need to be gradually withdrawn from the object so as to allow the object to exist on its own, independent from the self. The stress of this separation can be difficult for the ego to tolerate, and the pathological phantasy of being pushed out of the separate oedipal couple may make individuation feel like a banishment, an eternal void, or a lonely fragmentation. Therefore, the discovery of one's own unique identity is very fragile and prone to be experienced as a punishment, an impossible task, or a frightening lack of safety and nourishment. In these cases, the defensive urge is to eliminate difference, separation, or conflict.

Therefore, pleasing, submitting, and atoning can become a lifelong pattern in the search to return to the hoped-for reunion with the object or to find the lost object that never was there to begin with. Bion (1959) spoke of the interruption of this reunion, this journey back to the container, as experienced as a violent attack on the link essential for emotional survival.

So, for John and other patients like him, the idea of becoming separate and individual is at times exciting and wonderful but always layered with deep anxieties about the consequences to self and other. This anxiety is not always buffered by the belief in negotiation, forgiveness, understanding, compromise, and the idea of difference and disagreement being healthy or survivable.

John told me about how he spent the weekend with a new girlfriend he had met at a music concert. He told me he "really liked her; we got along like butter on toast." But, then he added that he was worried he "would get sucked in and trapped." In discussing this, he explained that he envisioned becoming obligated to please her and do "whatever it takes to make her happy," a familiar pattern in his life. John said, "After I do that old shoe for awhile, there is no me left. Now that I think of it, I don't know if there was ever a me to begin with. Whatever, Doc. I don't know what I am saying. Maybe I need to not smoke as much before I come here." I interpreted, "I think you just got in touch with some very uncomfortable feelings about how you want to have a self, but you feel you give it up to please us all, and when you turn away from us to find yourself, you aren't sure where you are." John replied, "Well, somehow you followed me through that mess and made sense of it." Here, he was describing my functioning as a beta container for his alpha state of confusion (Bion 1962b).

We went on to explore his ongoing anxiety over being separate in his mind while still present and in connection with me. I said, "To be yourself and to be relating with me is very difficult and new. You are not sure how to be with me without turning into a mirror of me or a servant to please me." John agreed and said he didn't want that to happen with this new girl, but he wasn't sure how to prevent it. But, then he associated to how he had gone downtown a few days ago for lunch and realized he was close to where he usually purchased drugs. He pulled his truck over and went to an ATM to check his bank account and see how much money he had to spend on drugs. He told me, "At that point, I realized I was trying to figure out how much money I had to throw away on getting crazy and that seemed crazy! So, I said No Way. I got back in the truck and went to get lunch. Close call."

I interpreted that he suddenly spoke up for himself and decided No Way, as opposed to how normally he "feels taken for a ride by his mind." This showed how he was suddenly more able and more willing to think for himself and share that independent thought with me. As a result of this successful step forward into autonomous thought and relating to me as more of an equal, he was able to associate to an even more risky area he normally kept secret. John "confessed" to really wanting to get the drugs because he was worried that if he were to "hook up with this new girl later on that day or on the weekend, he might not last." He gradually revealed that he has always harbored a fear of premature ejaculation with women and that he has come to believe that if he takes enough cocaine or narcotic, he can "last long enough to please her."

I interpreted that he was now willing to look at this fear in a new way and that maybe we together could figure out a better answer than the drugs. He said, "That sounds real good, but I am clueless. I can see that it sounds pretty bad that I want to score a bunch of crack or oxi to keep my dick up, but there you have it!"

Here, I felt the countertransference pull to comfort him and assure him this was OK and normal and that we would get through it together. But, I was also aware of how that would be an easy step toward me taking over and not having faith that by allowing him to have these insights, taking these risks to share himself, and trying to figure out better ways to cope with his anxiety, he could find his own answers and feel solid as an independent individual. John was in the moment able to comfort himself and use our relationship to find a way to soothe himself and work through these troubles. So, I avoided acting out the potentially crippling ideal father role and let him slowly grow into his own stronger self, along side of me as *he* determined how much of me he needed.

Regarding the fear of premature ejaculation, I interpreted that he was un-sure whether simply being himself with me, with this woman, or with anyone, would be enough to satisfy us, be accepted, or loved. Or, as he often feared, would we be disappointed and angry and reject him. I interpreted that he probably wanted to be loved for just who he was "as is," but didn't trust that being separate, different, and his own person was acceptable. John told me this "was the kettle of fish in his life and he never thought of any other way. But, maybe *we* could find a new way."

This was a pivotal moment in John's analytic progress, for two reasons. Usually, he put me into the role of the leader who had permission to be separate and express my individuality via interpretations. In response, he put himself into a dependent, neutral role of the follower and pleaser who had to carefully do my bidding or suffer the consequences of hurting me and/or being hurt in retaliation. But, now he was able to see us and allow us to be two separate people working together to find a solution. We both could contribute, and we both could have independent ideas that might blend together for a helpful mixture. So, this was a more mature depressive shift towards integration, hope, and trust in how the self and the object could exist.

In addition, this was an important moment in John's internal growth, mental cohesion, and coming together of normally split-off aspects of his mind. For years, he spoke of himself as a "we." So, instead of saying, "Yes, I now understand that, and I think I am managing some change in that," John would say, "Yes, we are now understanding that, and we think we are managing some changes." This was not just a unusual speech pattern but a symptom of his intra-psychic fragmentation in which it was not OK to have a coherent, independent self that spoke in unity. He suffered in such conflict and dealt with such great depressive phantasies that often had paranoid color to them, he was constantly attacking himself, slicing his ideas and feelings up into safe, non-conflictual piles, one for each situation. He was ready to be whatever you needed him to be. This resulted in a fragmented mind where there were so many pieces that he became a "we" instead of an "I." Now, in this mutative moment, he returned to a sense of unified self. This time when he said "we," he meant "you" and "I."

So, we are exploring his fear of independent identity resulting in being not enough and therefore hurting the object and possibly being hurt in return. His normal pattern was to prevent separation and encourage a symbiotic attachment where he merely shadowed the object, hoping to be loved for his ability to mirror. Normally, for John, the depressive position's opportunity of individuation as well as the appreciation of difference was experienced as more of a place of danger, collapse, failure, as well as abandonment, guilt, and persecution. As the result of our exploration, John seems much less anxious, has more of a choice in whether or not to use drugs and alcohol, and has more trust in survival of self and object after his emergence as a separate and independent individual. Regarding his worry about the new girl, I also interpreted that he was taking an independent risk in telling me that he wanted to see this new girl and explore their new relationship with me, despite what his parents had said about why he shouldn't.

In response, John said he really did want to "check it out and see how it all plays out, at least for now." He mentioned taking her to another music concert and momentarily backpedaled by saying, "Maybe it is a mistake to take her to the show. In the past, with other women, I have had to give up my fun time at the concert because I had to show them around and make sure they were having a good time. Maybe I wanted to chill out for awhile or go down to the river and take a swim between watching the bands. But, instead I had to hold her hand and be her goddamn guide for the day."

I interpreted that he had been telling me about how he likes this new girl and had his own hopes and excitement about being with her at the concert but now he was attacking it and making it a place where "he was trapped." So, I was interpreting the projective identification process in which he put these restrictive and punishing measures on his desire for a more separate and independent experience. After I made my comment, his anxiety seemed to reduce, and he said, "Well, maybe it won't be so bad. I think we could respect each other's needs to have our own thing—that could work. I remember when we went to the first concert, she was cool about it. I could go chill out at the bar, have a beer, and shoot the shit with the guys without having to worry about her, what she was doing, and what she needed. After a while I wondered over to the stage and found her dancing. I wasn't jealous or anything. I was relieved. She could enjoy herself and I could enjoy myself and then we could come back together and hang out and have fun with each other. That is so cool. OK. This has potential. I hope I don't fuck it up." I interpreted, "Either with drugs or with you getting scared of being yourself." John replied, "Yo. You got it!"

DISCUSSION

There are patients who struggle with primitive depressive phantasies about the object and their connection or lack of connection to that object. These patients often switch back and forth between identifying with the bad object, taking on the more demanding, aggressive, or impulsive nature of that object. Or, they more usually present as the unloved, passive, and anxious child that is seeking to please the object to avoid, rejection, abandonment, or attack. Indeed, this need to save, help, or please is often a complex mix of seeking attention, preventing damage, and avoiding conflict and anger. There is little trust of forgiveness, reparation, or understanding in any lasting manner.

In this clinical atmosphere, it is easy for the analyst to act out various roles within this phantasy, such as judgmental authority, loving and guiding parent, or controlling and directive know-it-all.

John's case represents a patient who for the most part feels in danger of hurting or being hurt by the object and tries to keep the peace by pleasing, advocating, and submitting. Only in mild verbal form and only rarely in interaction did John shift to an outright identification with the angry, rejecting, hurt object. For John, all the people in his life had their own lives and the right to express themselves freely. But, he did not allow himself that same right.

This censoring of any separation or individuation is the hallmark for patients such as John. These types of patients are struggling with primitive depressive reactions of guilt, fear, and anxiety. As evidenced by John's abrupt and early termination the first time in treatment, his drug and alcohol abuse, his extreme difficulty with relationships, and the general instability, dependency, sensitivity, and grave sense of emptiness in his life, the more borderline, paranoid-schizoid aspects of his personality were evident as well. This element of the precarious, slippery hold on the depressive position is common in these types of patients, who suffer with a very fragile foothold in the more stable realities of depressive functioning, and they instead frequently collapse into the paranoid-schizoid position. So, I was beginning to explore the internal anxiety and sense of emptiness John experienced if he didn't either identify with the aggressive tough guy image of his father and if he didn't fall back into the passive, pleasing little boy who wanted others to like him and not abandon him. Gradually, we are finding and building a new "we" for John, in which both self and object can coexist, thrive, and love. John is starting to believe he can operate separately and autonomously without harming others and without the risk of being banished or attacked by others.

5

Trouble in Paradise

The Trauma of Separation and Individuation within the Depressive Realm

Steiner (1984) notes that the total defensive organization that the patient uses to manage their internal experiences will be re-lived within the transference. As Joseph (1983) points out, the patient tries to utilize the analyst in particular ways that recruit us into these reincarnations of primitive infantile phantasy states. When patients in either the paranoid-schizoid position (Klein 1946) or more brittle immature states of depressive anxiety (Klein 1935) over-rely on projective identification and splitting, the countertransference can become a slippery area in which the analyst can interpretively act out and occasionally become the patient's wished-for ideal and/or dreaded opponent. Steiner (1984) goes on to clarify that modern Kleinian thinking sees projective identification as not only an unconscious phantasy but also a form of interpersonal and emotional action that affects the analyst, producing a state of mind that hopefully can be effectively understood in the countertransference and then used towards an interpretation.

However, sometimes we fail to detect such countertransference situations and act out the patient's projected desires, attacks, guilt, seductions, and fears. It has become a given in most psychoanalytic schools of thought that a certain degree of enactment is unavoidable but important to catch and hopefully utilize to better understand and assist the patient in their conflicts and struggles. Also, the Kleinian school has well documented that projective identification, the basis for most of these enactment scenarios, is not just used to attack, evacuate, or control, but also to communicate otherwise unbearable and unknown states of mind (Bion 1963; Rosenfeld 1971).

Steiner (1998) states that some patients use projective identification in an excessive manner to aggressively hand over their very identity, power, uniqueness, or autonomy. They tend to hand over, in phantasy and interpersonally, that about themselves that they imagine would create conflict and create separateness. So, they strive to create a persona of passivity and dependence, inviting the analyst to become guiding, parenting, or dominating. They push the analyst to think for them or to ignore them and replace their presence with the imprint of the analyst. This pushing of autonomy, opinion, and presence into the analyst can become aggressive and feel like an ongoing bombardment to the analyst, who in turn may react by quickly telling the patient what to do, how to think, or how their opinions are not as good as the analyst's. This domination can also come in the form of the analyst aggressively reassuring the patient that his opinions are fine and worthy, thereby providing the blessings and encouragement of the master onto the passive and meek follower. However, all these forms of enactment are usually very subtle and hard to track, thus easily becoming an insidious pattern in the transference/countertransference matrix.

The patients explored in this paper and illustrated by two cases show a desire for greater self-expression and separation from the object but also show a great reluctance to experiment with any true form of autonomy, separation, or growth. These anxieties regarding needing to please, to copy, and to follow all in the service of avoiding harm to or from the object emerge within the transference. Therefore, as Malcolm (1995) notes, that transference dynamic is the primary area to explore and interpret. The leading edge of the patient's anxiety regarding where they locate the thrust of their depressive phantasies is the other guidepost on how to interpret.

In other words, the analyst has to determine, at that moment, is the phantasy about the object or the self? Often, it is a confusing combination of both. These types of primitive depressive patients insist on striving to be the ideal, passive shadow as a way to please and avoid any separation or identity formation that could cause conflict. They see the object as either pleased, soothed, and temporarily appeased or hurt, offended, and out for revenge. In patients who are operating in this more fragmented depressive phantasy, internal experiences of separation or difference are felt as a loss of parts of the self, hence the resulting annihilation anxiety (Little 1966). Indeed, any move towards autonomy in the self is then seen as an extreme risk to the health and happiness of the object. Patients who are frightened about the consequences of growth, identity, and difference tend to engage the analyst in very complicated and layered transference states, fueled by splitting and projective identification, all colored and shaped by depressive phantasies.

Feldman (1992) notes that the analyst can become aligned with the patient in assessing or judging external objects or situations, such as trying to decide if a parent was cruel or unfair to the patient. In this process, the quality of the transference is ignored, and the manipulation of the patient to re-create a parental situation with the analyst is unseen. I would extend this idea to include all discussions of any external situations or individuals to potentially hold this distancing power, all possibly becoming a way to ignore the transference and, therefore, all a potential countertransference pitfall. Segal (1993b) notes that with excessive use of projective identification some patients lose sight of the reality of the analyst and feel completely in the grips of their phantasy object and through various forms of transference acting out, attempt to actualize certain phantasies in the transference. Segal notes that even depressive patients project in a very concrete and rigid manner, bringing the analyst to feel certain ways and often pushing him to act out in a subtle manner.

Melanie Klein (1940) noted that during the most intense depressive anxieties, the ego resorts to certain manic defenses, such as idealization and denial to deal with the terrible experience of "pining," a term Klein used to describe the difficult state of loss and mourning. The group of patients I am exploring are all desperately avoiding the loss of the ideal object and the persecution by the now bad object, so they try to deny any less than ideal state in themselves or their objects, hoping to maintain a conflict-free zone where peaceful and loving union always exists, but as illustrated by the case material that follows, at a great price. This price is the loss of individuality and autonomous thought and desire. Separation and difference are never experienced as safe, acceptable, helpful, or healthy. Dependency takes on a desperate and manipulative form while independence is to be hidden, secretly tasted, and publicly frowned on. Because of this intense struggle and conflict regarding growth, change, and personal identity, a great deal of projective identification is employed to protect the self and the object from these threatening phantasies.

When projective identification is so clearly the thrust of the transference, countertransference enactments are common.

As studied by modern Kleinians (Waska 2010c), countertransference acting out and interpretive enactments are difficult to avoid but important to understand and utilize. Sometimes, they may contribute to the demise of the treatment, which occurred in the first case, but the analyst must do their best to consistently self-analyze and manage these confusing feelings and thoughts that are triggered as the treatment occurs. Schoenhals (1996) notes that the creation of triangular mental space is the essence of successful oedipal and depressive growth. However, this moment in which the child experiences himself and his mind as separate from the object so important to him is extremely stressful and fraught with disaster. This sudden new experience of being separate, different, and autonomous and being aware of other separate, different, and autonomous objects can be threatening and felt as an assault, a loss, and a sudden betrayal.

At this point, there can be a collapse of triangular space. This occurred constantly in the first case and felt in the countertransference to be a possibility in the second case. In the process of analysis, the analyst becomes willing to contain (Bion 1962b) the patient's projections and allow the patient to become themselves within the analyst's mind. I believe these types of patients struggling with more primitive and immature aspects of the depressive position and suffering with conflicts concerning separation and autonomy refuse to allow the analyst into their mind, or, if they do, it is in a very restrictive manner, and they do not allow or tolerate the analyst to become a separate, different, or autonomous figure in their mind for very long without some sort of attack, loss, or collapse occurring.

CASE MATERIAL

This case demonstrates the delicate nature of the depressive position and the more primitive aspects of depressive functioning some patients struggle with. After seeing this patient for several years, the treatment came to an abrupt end by the patient's response to an enactment by the analyst which triggered the more persecutory and envious feelings concerning her conflicts with separation and individuation.

Sue was a young woman whom I saw on the couch, four times a week, for three years. During this time, we covered much ground and made a great deal of progress. Sue came to see me convinced she was capable of completely destroying her objects and bringing out the worst in all her relationships. She told me early on and reiterated it many times in many ways over the course of treatment, "I cannot be myself. If I were to stop paying attention to the other person and stop trying to please them and instead try to please myself or even to find myself, I will end up hurting everyone and then they will not love me. In fact, they will hate me." This was the core of the transference and ended up being the principle element in the projective identification process that eventually led to a series of enactments on my part that brought about the premature end of this treatment.

Sue was consumed with guilt over her feelings of always failing to please the object and instead hurting, disappointing, and offending the object. This very strong and ingrained phantasy about her power to collapse any viable relationship created a great deal of trouble in her life and generated a most difficult transference situation.

Sue had a history of dating men who were self-serving and not able or willing to communicate or see her as an equal. They always took the lead and pushed themselves into the spotlight, leaving Sue to feel lonely and forgotten. But, she would negate all of her unhappy feelings and blame herself for the lack of closeness and love. Therefore, she tolerated these sad conditions for long periods of time before she eventually broke the relationship off. One could say that this was the very phantasy that played out at the end of the treatment.

However, in examining the entire course of her analytic process, Sue mostly had the feeling that I was not happy with her, saw her as selfish and arrogant, and was sick and tired of dealing with her so I might reject or forget her at any given time. The idea that I was a man who was selfish or taking over the relationship with my needs was replaced by a phantasy of I was an important man who was bothered by her needs, her "stupid complaining," and her "unstable emotional bullshit." However, this switched back when the treatment came to an abrupt end. One can see that this vision of me as one more man who selfishly put himself over her and ignored her came back to life in a very intense way.

As far as the way this occurred in most of her dating life, we worked on this pattern quite a bit and things became much healthier. Sue started to find men who were more able to be open, see her as an equal, and contribute to a shared and loving relationship. However, this was a work in progress with many points of breakdown along the way.

In the transference, she was convinced I was always unhappy, disappointed, and hurt by her. For years, she almost begged me to agree with her terrible and negative self-image. This sadomasochistic method of relating grew in intensity at times to where Sue told me, "You hate me, I know it! I am sorry I am so stupid. Please don't get rid of me!" My attempts to explore her own possible feelings of anger, disappointment, or frustration at me went nowhere. For a period of time, her phantasy of me as this angry, rejecting object who could be hurt so easily and who needed to be pleased and controlled shifted into more of a romantic transference state. But, her underlying fear of rejection and abandonment remained. Sue told me, "Please don't push me away and forget me. To be forgotten is my greatest fear. I feel I could just vanish and drift away into little bits of dust if you don't keep me in your mind. I am convinced that one day you will just say you are done, finished with me. You will forget about me, and I will perish." I said, "You will no longer be in my heart or mind." She cried and said, "Yes. I won't exist inside you anymore." Based on the transference and the way Sue related to most people in her life, I consistently interpreted her fear of being her own person and how that would hurt others and cause them to turn on her or turn away from her. To be herself, separate and alive, was to ask to be forgotten or worse.

Over time, because of the intense projective identification dynamic Sue utilized, I found myself straying into small enactments. While many of her ways of relating to me were sexualized or romanticized and I was pulled into a flirty sort of being with her, the stronger undercurrent was mostly one of wanting me to be the leader, the wise and powerful father who told her whether she was doing well or doing poorly. So, when she arrived in a sexy outfit, she quickly told me she was sorry she had chosen to cut her hair that day and was sure I was repulsed by how horrible she looked and was going to quickly grow tired of her and her poor decisions.

Most of all, she created a transference of a judgmental person who could easily be hurt and driven to retaliation in the form of rejection unless she adhered to being a voiceless, passive, symbiotic creature. Independence and individuality were a threat to both of us. So, while I certainly interpreted the many sexually colored transference profiles and the outright night dreams and daydreams of having sex with me and living with me, I also interpreted these as being shaped by this passive follower scared by her own sense of self and her vision of me as needing her to be a certain way or there would be bloodshed on one side or another.

As mentioned, the intensity of the projective identification process was hard to handle at times, often affecting my interpretive stance. Sue would tell me a story about some recent activity at work in which she made some decision or a way she chose to interact with a friend or coworker. The overall message in how she told me the story was provocative in the sense that it lured me to suggest a better way of doing things or to basically question her opinion and judgment. I ended up in her business.

After I would make my comments, she would feel terrible and say she was "embarrassed to reveal how stupid she was and should know better than to tell me, a much more educated and wise person, her stupid and pathetic attempts at living." I would then feel bad and guilty in the countertransference, but I still tried to unravel the nature of what happened. Bit by bit, we discovered that she was essentially presenting stories of how she was being more assertive, decisive, or full of her own separate identity. Then, she sabotaged this new individual by displaying it in this masochistic manner, inviting me to judge it and push her with my "better and more educated opinion." So, Sue would step out into our relationship in a much more open and bold manner and then bring on an attack, through projective identification, to put herself back down to size by getting me to be the one to step in and take over the spotlight. This dynamic in reverse was part of how the treatment ended with a bang. During the bulk of the treatment, we were successful in interpreting, understanding, and working with many of these projective identification-induced transference/countertransference moments of acting out, but they did go on and sometimes restricted the otherwise genuine progress towards her becoming more comfortable and confident with her own identity, feelings, and thoughts.

Throughout the analytic treatment, I interpreted at certain times that Sue was probably harboring a great deal of anger and disappointment toward her objects that she projected onto. However, it was only toward the end of the third year that she was able to accept, tolerate, and share some of those feelings. But, usually when she did, an act of self-definition and inserting herself into the relationship rather than standing on the sidelines waiting for me to lead, she would quickly attack and neutralize them by apologizing and undoing them with excuses and self-blame. Still, in her relationships, whether at work, in romance, or in the transference, she began to have some sense of self-agency and expression of positive and negative feelings. So, things were progressing but still in a rocky manner, with frequent primitive depressive episodes of extreme guilt, remorse, and conviction of being unacceptable and sure to be thrown out and forgotten at a moment's notice. The transference remained one of an idealized state in which I was close to pulling the trigger on my love and unleashing hate instead. However, there were a few cracks along the way when she told me she was angry that I was late to the session and that she felt I was "shorting her of her property." I interpreted this as a new risk of stating she actually had property and was willing to express her desire to keep her property and even defend it. She would usually apologize for her comments and in the process negate or ignore what I was saying.

Sue's anger and her need to control me came out during a few different sessions over the years, all threaded together by the same intolerance for separation or individual need apart from the other. When I came out to get her from the waiting room, there were many times when Sue was "convinced that I was angry and intolerant of her, still sick of her from some prior session." Other times, she was "really worried because she could tell I looked sad and distant as we came into the office. It must be something she has done or if it is something she didn't do, maybe I need her to leave and give me the time to regroup and rest."

During several sessions, I would make a noise drinking from a plastic water bottle or shift in my chair a certain way that left her immediately alarmed and certain that I was either upset, angry, or depressed. She would not take no for an answer during these moments, and I interpreted that she pushed me in the corner without any other way of being in her mind. I was angry, hurt, or disappointed and that was that. Here, I was interpreting the aggressive control and rigid projections she made without any allowance for difference, change, or individual uniqueness in me.

A similar situation occurred several times over the years when we would spend some time talking on the phone because she was in crisis or because I was out of town and she felt the need to still meet. During some of these calls, Sue heard a noise, be it the sound of a piece of paper I was moving, a bag I was moving so as to clear some space at the desk I was sitting at, or my dog barking in the background. When this reality aspect of my life suddenly entered her orbit, she was intensely upset. She would immediately tell me she could "tell I didn't have the time for her, was busy so she was sorry for bothering me, or that I obviously needed to take care of something so she would get off the phone." Then, I would have to reassure her, convince her, and prove to her that I was indeed attentive and fine enough to take her on. Here, I again interpreted her need to control me and force me into a few limited and very rigid images of someone who was too busy for her, too preoccupied with myself to notice her, or someone too overburdened to take her needs on. My individuality, announced by my unique and separate noises that broke the mold of a mirror reflection completely in tune and the same as her, was alarming and unacceptable. So, she attacked it in a sadomasochistic fashion, usually taking on the role of apologetic violator, but also making me out to be the bad guy by being too weak and overwhelmed, too depressed, too angry, and/or so forth. But, I had no choice. She controlled me and shoved me into that category without any room for exploration or curiosity, or variance. I think that is the same feeling Sue ended up experiencing when I intruded into her life by speaking for about five minutes about what I did over the weekend, which happened to be in a location somewhat close to where she lived.

So, this all came into fiery focus during one session in the fourth year of analysis. I see it as a combination of my ongoing enactment of every once in awhile inserting myself as an independent, separate character into the private world of her mind and her idea of us as a sadomasochistic pair in which even though she or I dominate, neither one is allowed to have much self-definition. So, over the years, I think I acted out against this prohibition by making comments about theory when she asked, answered questions she had about Freud with my own personal monologue, said a few words about my new car after she said she noticed it, and sharing facts about the farmer's market I some-times shop at. While a certain degree of acting out or interpretive enactment is often unavoidable, it is always an issue to be aware of, and never assume the patient is unaffected. Especially with narcissistic or borderline patients, including those who suffer with these more primitive depressive phanta-sies, these more personal acknowledgments can easily become part of the patient's precarious hold on reality that easily falls back into the depths of primitive guilt, persecution, or sadomasochistic withholding and exhibition. The other danger is that these types of patients can be so in conflict when it comes to difference, independence, and separation that they become envious of those who show that quality and feel deprived and/or intruded upon when around those individuals who own that sense of freedom without being tied to guilt and persecution regarding union and individuation.

So, we were discussing Sue's plan to have her new boyfriend over to join her at an office party and he said he didn't think it was "proper" as he had been a manager of that department at one point and said he thought things "should be kept on a professional basis." The way Sue described it was logical and in agreement with him, but I sensed she was keeping back some other more disappointed or frustrated feelings. When I inquired, she at first denied it and said he made sense and she respected his choices, that it was a "professional workplace situation."

In the countertransference, I noticed myself feeling angry with the boyfriend for seeming to be so controlling, uptight, or unreasonable. So, I asked Sue if she might find it hard to express to me the full spectrum of how she felt, rather than keep the peace with me and the boyfriend by being so understanding. Sue told me, "Well, I do feel kind of frustrated and like he is setting up rules. I just want to have him by my side. I am trying to do things for him and with him, and lately I have really tried to put myself out there and show him my real identity and not hide and try and just make him happy. I am trying to share more of me." I said, "So, his saying no to your invitation felt like a bit of a rejection of you?" She replied, "Yes. It did. But, I am trying to be understanding. Like I said, I am trying to share my likes and interests with him. I just invited him to this special little restaurant in my neighborhood. It will be a surprise because they specialize in authentic South American food, which I really enjoy, and I want to share that with him. It is a really neat little place, very colorful, down a few blocks from my apartment."

Now, over the course of the last year, Sue had told me a great deal about her apartment, including the general layout, where she slept (which included phantasies of us sleeping together), how she sunbathed in her bikini on the porch, and all about her cooking in the kitchen. I interpreted she wanted me to enter into her world and be with her and that even though she was very timid, reserved, and sure of punishment if she dared to show off in any way, she also was willing to take the risk to flirt with me in this shy, teasing sort of way. Sue also had described her favorite activities in her neighborhood with many colorful stories, telling me about the gym she went to every other day and the local park she liked to hang out in. Sue told me she had gotten to know a few of the locals and enjoyed being recognized by a few regulars at the park. Here, she described how much she enjoyed the neighborhood and how "I feel grown up, happy, and in my own kind of place. It just feels like me." This phrase is important because in what happened next I think Sue suddenly felt like it went from feeling like me, separate and autonomous, to feeling like her analyst, invaded and taken over, without her own identity. In her mind, her property was taken over and made into my property.

It just so happened that the day before this particular session, I had gone to that general area of the city for the first time to have lunch. While my office is in the city, I only come into the city to work and very rarely come over for pleasure. But, a friend had invited me to have lunch and walk around the tourist part of that section of town. So, I was now full of visual information about the area Sue had told me about for the past year. When she told me about the special restaurant and its general location, I asked if it was by XYZ Street. Sue said, "Have you been by there recently?" I replied, "Yes. I went there yesterday for the first time for lunch. It is a beautiful area. Are the places you tell me about around there?"

For the next five minutes or so, we exchanged details about it. I found myself going on and on like an excited tourist. Then, Sue said, in a sudden, tense, angry, and anxious outburst, "Please stop talking about yourself! I want you to stop talking about yourself." After a moment of tension, alarm, and anger that was very strong in the very silent office room, I said, "OK. I can see what you mean. I am sorry to take up all the airspace. What are you feeling about it?" Sue told me that she was tired of when I "talked too much about myself." She mentioned times when she would bring up some situation which involved a location she visited, a type of artist that she enjoyed, a movie she had seen, or a decision she had made at work. Then, I would make my interpretations about what her conflicts might be or what the transference struggle seemed to be, but I would also be adding my "own two cents" about the actual external topic. I asked her if she felt I was trespassing on her and making her feel like it was my session instead of hers. She told me it "felt wrong for you to talk about yourself so much, and everything seems upside down right now."

The next session, Sue told me she was "taking a break to think it all over, and she needed to put up some space between us and have time to distance herself from me." I said, "It sounds like it scared you when I said I was near where you live, like I was invading your space. I am sorry if that is how it felt. I hope we can talk about it and try to understand this so you can feel safer and

OK." She said she wasn't sure if she wanted to and didn't know if she would even be returning. In fact, she called the next day and said she was "not coming back and to take me off the books." Despite my reaching out to Sue with two calls to ask her if she would like the chance to talk about her feelings some more, she never called me back.

In reviewing my actions and the entire treatment, I came to several conclusions. Through projective identification and countertransference dynamics, I think Sue constantly put her unwanted and scary feelings of independence, opinion, strength, and separation into me and other men. So, for awhile, she felt secure and safe being with a man who defined things, lead the way, and told her what was right and what was wrong. I certainly fell into this along the way but also interpreted this transference throughout the treatment. As a result, there was substantial change in this area but obviously not in totality. Of course, this security was also a straight jacket, as she then felt she had to follow, like a passive servant, the will and way of the master or she would be punished and abandoned. Indeed, for Sue and other patients who also suffer from these more primitive depressive phantasies, the primal threat is to be forgotten and rejected because by becoming separate and individual, they imagine forgetting and rejecting their objects. Sue's own anger, desire for power, and sense of self came out in her masochistic ownership of "being the greatest disappointment to my therapist," the "worst patient," the "most crappy friend to all her friends," and the "most miserable girlfriend to every one of her boyfriends." In these ways she could be unique and special without too much threat from the object, but to strive to be happy, unique, and defined by her own thoughts and feelings in a healthy positive manner was a danger to self and other.

Looking back at the incident where I brought up my visit to her neighborhood, I think several issues occurred in the countertransference that were triggered by certain projective identification processes. Without spelling it out, Sue was upset that her boyfriend called the shots and felt strong enough to define the boundaries of what he wanted and what he didn't want and express it without any concern or worry. I think she was envious of any person, especially men like myself and her boyfriend, who could act independently and feel OK saying or doing what they wanted without fear of reprisal. Separation and individuation were all around her, but she excluded herself from that freedom, so she felt resentful and envious of others who had that freedom.

When she indicated she thought her boyfriend was "being a little unfair" but that she "understood and could see his point," I think she was angry and envious of him defining their relationship and defining her own sense of self without her feeling she had any say in it. This was the same pattern, yet hardly as severe, as she had experienced in all her relationships. In the countertransference, I felt a sense of outrage and injustice for her because she could not own that fully herself. I think I ended up acting that countertransference feeling out by unconsciously saying, "I will show you that it is perfectly OK for us to hang out in the same place even though it is your neighborhood. I am flexible and OK with it unlike your uptight boyfriend. We can talk about these mutual interests without having to deal with all these silly professional boundaries." In other words, I was trying to prove to her I could be a better boyfriend and that it was OK for me to be in her workplace/neighborhood without the rules. So, I think I became the part of Sue that wanted to break through the oedipal barrier she felt so constricted by and assert her independence and autonomy without having to always answer to others. But, when she saw me doing that, the other side of her conflict came through, and she reacted with immediate outrage and a sense of violation. All the rules came out again, and I was punished in the way she always feared. I was rejected, abandoned, banished, and forgotten. Ultimately, Sue still had to reject our mutual individuality by shoving us into our rigid boxes of disappointer and disappointed, of self and object locked into predicable roles demanded by each other. While my enactment was certainly not helpful to the overall treatment, it was by itself or even as part of a small pattern not enough to derail the sense of safety and trust for many patients. But, for Sue and other patients who are fragile and barely managing themselves at the edge of these more primitive depressive struggles over independence and slavery, my acting out was too much to bear.

Overall, Sue's treatment was a successful one but one in which the remaining core emotional issues came out during my lapse in therapeutic judgment, extinguishing the chance for us to continue our journey to psychological change. It is the difficult position for both analyst and patient to find a way to work together when change is possible but seen as a threat to self and object. These terrible phantasies can become activated within intense projective cycles to create situations in which even after a great deal of progress is made and trust is built, one non-ideal incident can spell the end. This is the constant cloud that looms over the treatment when these delicate and frightening issues of depressive anxiety over separation, autonomy, abandonment, and persecutory guilt remain as a constant companion to the transference.

So, it is frustrating to see this stormy abrupt termination after years of painstaking progress. Sue made many important and vital changes in her internal and external life over the years of analyst work. She went from working as a secretary and feeling inferior and incapable in most ways to returning to graduate school and entering the field of science where she immediately proved her skill and intelligence as an intern. Sue took up exercise and began to honor her body more, rather than see it as a "pile of fat without definition." As mentioned, her choice of men went from narcissistic individuals who were so self-defined that they totally eclipsed Sue's personal identity and they usually ignored her needs or opinions to men who respected her, encouraged her to be her own person, and asked for her thoughts on matters. Relationships became more of a shared mutuality with two individuals being separate but unified. The depression, constant crying, intense masochistic self-hatred, and severe anxiety Sue lived with when entering treatment all shrunk to a much more manageable state of doubt and apprehension over situations when she wanted to or needed to become more individuated and strong in her own accord.

It seems that on one hand, I managed to replicate some of her ongoing conflicts and fears regarding these states of becoming separate and defining a true sense of self. But, I believe that even though my enactments caused her to terminate the treatment, we accomplished a great deal. Perhaps, Sue was ready to separate from me and try things on her own, and this was the only way to cut those ties. At the same time, perhaps I prevented her from achieving even more growth and individuation. Could it be that once I acted out the phantasy of yet another man preventing her from being an equal or having a sense of privacy and integrity, by leaving me she once and for all was able to feel OK about separating, individuating, and saying good-bye without fear of revenge or unbearable guilt? Finally, the phantasy that I was somehow saying yes to her oedipal wishes and her flirtatious description of where she lived and what she wore in the intimate confines of her apartment was too close for comfort, and she had to turn the tables on me. As mentioned in the beginning of this case, Sue came into treatment feeling angry with self-serving men who used her and ignored her needs and self-definitions. She tolerated this for so long and then got rid of the men. She then felt very guilty and blamed herself, and the cycle started all over again. Once in treatment, she shifted from being angry at these aloof men in power to the fear that I was now her, the victim of her ugly, selfish, hurtful ways. In the end, she turned back to the feeling of being sick of tolerating a careless man and once again picked up and moved on. In between, she had worked hard and grown into a much more separate and differentiated woman, proud of herself in many ways and I believe ready to take that with her without feeling she had to discard toxic material or confess to stolen merchandise.

In conducting analytic treatment with patients who struggle with such severe internal conflicts around grief, persecution, loss, and emotional collapse, it is frequent that trust breaks down, hope becomes fragile, and growth stalls out. I know I could have done better and I feel I should have done better. But, I also think we did very well together and managed to establish a level of functioning and vision never dared before in her life. So, regardless of the disorganized and messy nature of things along the way and the fiery end to it all, there was significant change. I think Sue could now trust a bit more the idea that being herself did not mean harm to herself or others. This may be the end of Sue's treatment encounter with me but only the beginning of a much fuller life with herself and her future objects.

CASE MATERIAL

During the third year of David's analytic treatment, following my announcement that I would be away for a week, he told me, "I will be away the week before your vacation, so I will see you after you get back." I replied, "You say that very matter-of-factly. I wonder what feelings go with that or what feelings have been put aside?" Since David was prone to being very intellectual and using logic to cut off his feelings, this was a fairly regular interpretation I made to begin exploring why he felt he had to be a certain controlled way with me. During the first two years, part of how I acted out the projective identification-induced countertransference was merely go along with his long, detailed, concrete monologues in which he was really trying to impress me, control me, and provide evidence that he was following what he thought was my demand that he talk about certain topics and look at certain psychological patterns in his life. This left me to be the quiet, potentially angry, dominating leader whom he wished to please and create a very fragile alliance in which I was the proud, happy father of my hard-working boy whom I would always care for. But, this ideal could easily crumble in his mind, depending on how he was delivering the goods and how I was accepting them. This one-way dynamic was similar to the first case of Sue in that David was always on the verge of feeling he would disappoint me early in the treatment process. Later on, it shifted to him now being the one who was disappointed, rejected, and no longer willing to participate. With David, my pattern of enactment was not so much as to talk too much about myself in reaction to the seductive sadomasochistic transference, as to become underinvolved, feeling bored with the more obsessive, rigid transference in which he neutralized us with details and facts. However, as with the case of Sue, I did my best to notice my countertransference reactions and make appropriate interpretations with the information I gained.

So, David responded to my question about his lack of interest in us not meeting for two weeks by saying, "The way I see this relationship has changed. I used to think I would get something very special and complete out of it and I used to see you in a certain way. But, now that has all changed. So, if we don't meet for a few weeks, I am OK with it. I don't feel I will miss anything critical, and I don't feel I owe it to you anymore." Here, in the countertransference, I felt similar to when the first patient, Sue, told me to "stop talking about myself" and that she "didn't like to be with me anymore; it doesn't feel right." I was braced for a fallout and wondered how my sudden and dramatic shift in their mind would affect us and what my fate might be. I understand this to be the reverse of the normal projective identification transference in which for the most part of the treatment with both patients, they saw me as ready to shift at any moment and see them as disappointing, wrong, or bad. Either way, they would be no longer necessary and no longer wanted. So, for Sue, her ultimate dread was to "be forgotten and thrown out," and David had told me in the second year of treatment that his lifelong dread was "to not be noticed, not be loved, to have no worth." He said, "As you know, my father was brutal. He hit me, he slapped me, and he kicked me. He made me literally lick his boots. But, the worst of it was feeling he turned his back on me, betrayed me, and no longer was there as the father I wanted."

So, I responded to David by saying, "You sound both relieved and a bit sad or disappointed that I am no longer the person you wished for." David said, "It is all of the above, but I am dealing with it now. Just trying to accept that this is not what I hoped for or expected." I replied, "When did I disappoint you, when did we fall from grace?" Here, I interpreted the shift from ideal pair or ideal object. I did so to help clarify exactly how he saw the shift in his mind. He said, "Ever since the incident with the insurance company, I have felt let down and disappointed. I have come to realize you are not the person I thought you were, that you don't care for me no matter what. You do care but not in that no-matter-what way. You let me down."

Here, in the countertransference, I felt a sense of dread and realized my place as an ideal object in his mind was falling apart. Throughout the treatment, much like the case of Sue, I was placed in a position of authority, power, and wisdom. But, this narrow character function also assigned me in phantasy an intimidating, dominating, demanding, and self-focused role in which my obligated followers had to please me and make sure they followed my bidding. They had to make sure to not disappoint me or let me down. To do this, they were in a difficult position as they felt the need to subjugate their individuality to allow me to be the captain with all things. So, they tried hard to hide any unique personal thoughts or feeling that might be seen as separate or in disagreement with me out of fear of offending me or challenging me as not the only person in town with a separate and autonomous mind.

David's fear of his own identity and exposing and expressing his unique self was evident in many ways. He had a very difficult time signing his name to checks or documents. This came up one time when he was writing me a check and he had to pause and make a really concentrated effort to sign his name. I asked him what the difficulty was. David explained, "I think I am so used to trying to sign my name so that each person will be happy and that the signature is the appropriate one for whatever the situation is that I end up having more than one signature that I could write. But, then I get confused which one is which and how to write it."

I interpreted, "Another way of saying that might be that you are very uncomfortable being yourself with me, signing in as yourself without trying to figure out what I might need or want." He agreed and associated to other ways he ends up stuck after trying to figure out the best way to be for the other. I commented that he is trying so hard to control us and make sure I end up feeling a certain way about him that we become a prisoner of that control. Here, I was introducing the idea that not only was he trying to please me to mitigate any possible harm to him or to me, but that he in fact was not just a victim but an active contributor and author of this intense anxiety by trying to control us and make me be a certain way.

Getting back to the way he felt I was no longer who he wished me to be and how he felt disappointed, that particular issue came about because he was using health insurance to pay for the visits, and after switching health care plans, he needed to call the insurance company and ask for a new "authorization code" to activate his mental health coverage with me. A few weeks went by with David not remembering to call. I reminded him a couple of times, and when he finally did, he was told the new authorization code would begin that very day and it could not be backdated. He told me that and asked for advice. I told him he should try and get them to backdate it, but if they would not, he would have to pay for those two weeks out of pocket. When he called them back, they told him they could not backdate it, but if I went to their website, I could manually do it myself. I told David, "That was ridiculous"—how could a provider do that when they as the actual company can't? He called again, and again they told him I needed to do it on the website.

When David told me this, my countertransference was made up of several components. First of all, I was sick of having to deal with the endless and enormous amount of absurdity that is part of working with insurance companies. So, this time I was somewhat lashing out with frustration when I said, "I am sorry, but I don't have the time to waste with that. I can pretty much guarantee that is not the way it works. If I can change the dates on their website, they of course could do the same. I understand you were not in their computer system for those two weeks because your company didn't provide them with the data in time, but that is not my fault or yours. But, maybe if you had called earlier they could have put it in. However, I don't see why they can't backdate it. Bottom line, I don't want to do that because I know it will be a waste of my time, and I don't have that time to waste. I am sorry, but it isn't my fault and it isn't your fault but that is the way it is."

At the same time, I was being genuinely honest with David about how I felt and what personal stand I needed to take. When I did so, I felt a small twinge of tension and guilt, but I also felt good about standing up for myself. This last part is important because I believe it was part of a projective identification process in which David gave me certain unwanted, uncomfortable states of mind but also wasn't sure if he wanted me to exercise them or simply bury them or destroy them. The details of this came out later in the following session.

He started off the session talking about how bad he felt for his girlfriend who "had been going through some tough times lately. She has put on lots of weight, and it is partly due to her not working out because of her back problems and partly because she has been so overwhelmed by trying to figure out her next career move. I have tried really hard to support her by suggesting we go for a run or inviting her to go to the gym." David went on for some time talking about the various ways he was trying to be supportive and coming up with ideas to help her get in shape and feel better about herself.

In the countertransference, I sensed that while he was emphasizing what a nice supportive boyfriend he was being, I felt he was hiding his more frustrated self from me. I interpreted that he might be upset that she was getting fat and he was not happy about it because it didn't please him. But, he felt he had to appear as a totally selfless person to me or I would be disappointed in him. So, he had to neutralize his own autonomous mind and present this prepackaged image to me instead. David said, "I feel you just caught me being bad. I feel very guilty feeling that way, but it is true. I don't like her fat. I want her to go to the gym or something and start losing that weight. I don't want a fat girlfriend, but I feel so wrong feeling that and saying that. In fact, I feel very selfish like I only am looking out for myself and not being nice to her." I interpreted that he wants to be the ideal, all-caring one without any identity or stance of his own, just like he wanted me to be the ideal, selfless object with him.

David said, "That is exactly why I am upset about the insurance mess. I wanted you to just be this pure person who made it all better, but then you actually had an opinion of your own, and I couldn't stand it. I don't want you to have a self, I want you to be this pure thing there only for me." I interpreted, "It is very painful to realize that and acknowledge that you actually have separate wants and needs that may or may not be in line with me or her. It is hard to let me be my own person in your mind without feeling disappointed, hurt, or angry." David said, "It is really tough, but I am limping ahead because deep down I know that is exactly what I need to embrace. I want to be myself and finally believe that everyone else will be OK with it. No one has to perish because I introduce myself to the world. I won't get punished, and I don't have to feel guilty." Here, this is the painful, difficult, but extremely important growth in the direction of more mature depressive functioning in which both self and object get to exist as separate, different, and autonomous beings but still together and able to respect and love each other.

III

STRIVING FOR ANALYTIC CONTACT UNDER DIFFICULT CONDITIONS

Doing the Best We Can

Establishing Analytic Contact with Non-Attachment Patients

The influence of the media prejudice, the overall culture disinterest, and the ever-tightening restrictions of the managed care industry make for a formidable and sometimes near impossible climate in which to practice psychoanalysis. The field of psychoanalysis has been under attack and crumbling for many years, but only recently has this crisis been acknowledged by the members themselves. I have documented much of the research and literature in my previous publications (Waska 2005, 2006, 2007, 2010a, 2010b, 2010c, 2010d). These findings show that the typical psychoanalyst, after graduating his or her training, has at most one patient in four to five times a week on the couch analysis. Most graduated and certified analysts have a practice filled with patients who only come once or twice a week, sometimes using the couch. These are patients with grave mental disturbances including personality disorders combined with anxiety and depressive problems. Many have additional alcohol or drug problems. It is not unusual for the patient to enter treatment seeking help with collapsing marriages. In these cases, the treatment becomes couples therapy conducted by a psychoanalyst trying to work with two individuals in a last-ditch effort to find immediate relief from the culmination of years of conflict. So, the idealized, stereotypical portrayal of an analyst with many high-functioning neurotic patients being seen on the couch five times a week for years is just not happening in this day and age.

The overall crisis in psychoanalysis, the decline in patients seeking high-frequency in-depth treatment, and the reduction in candidates applying to training institutes goes back to the '80s and '90s. For example, Schafer (1997), in discussing trends in the field as pertains to practice in the United States, notes that there is great concern in simply trying to maintain an analytic practice. He says these problems stem from changes in insurance coverage, alternative therapies that promise fast relief without much mental exploration, and the general decline in the economy. A year later, Tyson (1998) noted the problems to be "profound and worldwide" with challenges that are "immense." These concerns had already prompted the International Psychoanalytic Association to form an ad hoc committee to investigate the issues back in 1994. The committee issued its findings in 1997 in their report entitled "Welcome to the Crisis" (Engelbrecht 1997). The report noted that the worldwide economic situation is partly to blame. Sadly, this part of the picture is become much graver since the report was written. They found a decline in patients overall, and the patients who do seek treatment with a psychoanalyst are more interested in short-term treatments than long-term analysis. They also note a decline in interest in psychoanalytic training. In 2009, the largest and oldest psychoanalytic institute in San Francisco decided for the first time in many years to not have a new class of candidates because the numbers of applicants were so few.

The idea of psychoanalysis as something outdated, without verifiable results, elitist, and rigid in its application continues to grow among the general public as well as within the therapeutic community. Most graduates of psychoanalytic training institutes rarely see patients more than once or twice a week and rarely on the couch. As mentioned, research starting in the '90s shows the graduating analyst to have only one patient in traditional psychoanalysis, if that. Couples therapy and low-frequency individual therapy are the norm.

However, the need for a rigorous treatment that addresses the core, unconscious conflicts that can choke a person's view of life and poison their way of seeing themselves and others will never be outdated or unneeded. While the academic debate over the differences between psychoanalysis and psychoanalytic psychotherapy continue to take up space in journals and time in workshops, the reality on the ground is much more clear and straightforward. Patients need help with their deepest psychological turmoil, and the essentials of Freud's and Melanie Klein's work remain a vital and tremendously effective method of providing that help and emotional transformation.

However, the current reality of private practice and clinic practice is difficult, rocky, and sometimes quite bleak. Research indicates that patients fall into three categories regarding how long they tend to stay in treatment. A high proportion of patients stop after three to five visits, the second group after five to ten, and the third group manage to continue for longer periods of time. So, while we hope to see all patients in long-term treatment, only a third of those who show up at our door will enter into an enduring psychological exploration. When examining the trends in how patients terminate, similar patterns emerge. Approximately one third of all patients terminate in a healthy, mutually agreed upon manner after working through much of their issues. Another third leave due to circumstantial factors, such as having to move, suffering a job loss, a sudden change in insurance coverage, or troubles with childcare. This group of patients usually has made significant progress in their emotional work, but things are left unfinished.

The last group terminates abruptly, after usually minimal progress or after a period of growth followed by a massive regression, and they leave in a manner that usually acts out the core transference anxieties. To truly study the nature of our analytic work, we must explore all three of these clinical situations. The literature tends to focus more on the first group and rarely on the second or third. The two cases presented in this paper highlight the third group in the hopes of showing how difficult our work can be, how the analyst method is still valuable in such troubling circumstances, and how we can still practice as analysts even in such apparently non-analyst situations.

My belief is that our therapeutic approach must be one that applies the psychoanalytic techniques of Melanie Klein and her contemporary followers to the real world of treating patients in private practice and clinic settings. This may mean some modification of technique, but by and large it is the adaptation of the same fundamental principles used in traditional Kleinian work to the treatment of all patients, regardless of frequency, diagnosis, or external circumstance. In previous publications, I have described this as the establishment of Analytic Contact. We all strive to create a psychoanalytic process with each patient, but this is a dynamic that can come and go within the same session, depending on transference and countertransference factors. When we break down this process to the moment-to-moment interactions, on an intra-psychic level, between patient and analyst, we are examining the Analytic Contact that is either taking place or being avoided. So, if we are able to string consistent moments of analytic contact together and maintain that clinical climate, we have created an enduring psychoanalytic process.

Some patients will not tolerate this process for very long. However, even in short, aborted treatments with disturbed patients, analytic contact can be established in temporary measure. Whether we can maintain this or if it is disrupted and discouraged by the patient or analyst is a measure of how well we can consistently provide mutative interpretations of the total transference, contain and utilize our countertransference, and trace it back to the projective identification cycles that are present. And, it is a measure of how well the patent can or is willing to tolerate the experience of facing their internal conflicts and allowing themselves to be in the analyst mind and the analyst in their mind without resorting to exaggerated ways of fleeing, defending, and denying the nature of their core object relational phantasies.

In broadening Klein's work to match today's clinical climate (Waska 2005, 2006, 2007), I still advocate always attempting to engage the patient in an exploration of their unconscious phantasies, transference patterns, defenses, and internal experience of the world. Regardless of frequency, use of couch, length of treatment, or style of termination, the goal of psychoanalytic treatment is always the same: the understanding of unconscious phantasy, the resolution of intra-psychic conflict, and the integration of self/object relations, both internally and externally. The psychoanalyst uses interpretation as their principal tool, with transference, countertransference, and projective identification being the three clinical guideposts of those interpretive efforts. Viewed from the Kleinian perspective, most patients utilize projective identification as a psychic cornerstone for defense, communication, attachment, learning, loving, and aggression. As such, projective identification constantly shapes and colors both the transference and countertransference.

By attending to the interpersonal, transactional, and intra-psychic levels of transference and phantasy with consistent here-and-now and in-the-moment interpretation, the Kleinian method can be therapeutically successful with neurotic, borderline, narcissistic, or psychotic patients, whether being seen as individuals, couples, or families and at varied frequencies and duration.

The Kleinian method of Analytic Contact strives to illuminate the patient's unconscious object relational world, gradually providing the patient a way to understand, express, translate, and master their previously unbearable thoughts and feelings. We make analytic contact with their deepest experiences so they can make personal and lasting contact with their full potential.

Successful analytic contact involves not only psychic change, but a corresponding sense of loss and mourning. So, every moment analytic contact is both an experience of hope and transformation as well as dread and despair as the patient struggles with change and a new way of being with himself and others. Successful analytic work always results in a cycle of fearful risk taking, hasty retreats, retaliatory attacks, anxious detours, and attempts to shift the treatment into something less than analytic, something less painful. The analyst interprets these reactions to the precarious journey of growth as a way of steering the treatment back to something more analytic, something that contains more meaningful contact with self and other. The support that we give our patients includes the inherent vow that we will help them survive this painful contact and walk with them into the unknown. The following two cases show the attempt to establish analytic contact, the difficulties maintaining it, and the patient's ultimate disruption, rejection, and destruction of that contact.

CASE MATERIAL

Tony came to see me because his wife of five years was ready to divorce him if he didn't "find a way to start opening up, be more of a man, and less of a robot." She wanted him to be much more sexual and much more communicative than he had been. They had tried some couples therapy that "didn't work," and she was now in individual therapy. Her therapist had recommended that Tony see someone himself. When I heard about his wife's view of him, I was interested because of my own immediate reaction to meeting with Tony. Here, I was noticing my countertransference as well as the manner in which Tony was presenting himself to me in the transference. O'Shaughnessy (1983) notes that Klein helped us understand how the dynamics of the transference are always a series of object-related, unconscious, and interactional events and that our interpretations should therefore always be about the interaction of the patient and analyst at an intra-psychic level.

So, I interpreted, "You seem to describe it all in a way that makes it so you are sent here by her, for me to decide what is best for you. Two people telling you what to do and you not having much of a say." Tony responded, "Well,

I want her to not leave me, and you are supposed to know how to change what people do." So, here I was listening to how he responded to my interpretation and noted the combination of desperation in his message and the condescending tone of how he described me as a service that changes people without them needing to be involved in the process. I felt like responding to this in an irritated or condescending way, a payback of sorts. Instead, I managed to simply contain his projections into me and my reactions to them. Containment is often a type of silent interpretation (Schafer 1994a) that is necessary in many clinical situations, especially tense ones such as this where there is not much else known for now and to say more would probably be more of an enactment (Anderson 1999) than anything else.

Very quickly, I noticed it was like trying to get blood out of a stone. I use this metaphor because I think that was the type of sadistic and persecutory transference phantasies Tony had which he brought to life through projective identification. With Tony's stonewalling approach of not relating to me or to himself, I was left to try and drag out any sort of evidence of life within him. Communication seemed too dangerous, so Tony attacked it and avoided it. He remained emotionless to the point of extreme indifference and then took my attempts to understand him as sadistic attacks (Schafer 1994b).

Tony slowly and reluctantly disclosed a lifelong feeling of "being on the outside with no clue of how to interact with other people, especially how everyone seems to enjoy just talking for the sake of it, with no real point to it." After a long and painful, to me, pause, he continued, "I guess I am hoping you will show me how to interact with other people and make it look like I belong, so at least I can make my wife stay." Tony said this in an eerie way that made me feel like he was an alien from space wanting a manual on how to sneak in and blend into society but not really wanting to give up his alien citizenship, instead simply trying to stave off his wife's rejection. So I said, "You are not sure you want any part of it? It is just for others and just to keep her around?" Tony said, "That is the main reason, yes." Hoping to hear something about his internal struggles but instead hearing this concrete, robot-like response, I felt suddenly hopeless and wanting to either give up or somehow convince him to open up and stop being so controlling and cautious. This countertransference again showed me Tony's intense attacks on attachment and defenses against partaking in relatedness and aliveness were being projected. He also spoke with disdain and spite about how people "like to get into stupid conversations about nothing. I don't see the point, and I have never been able to do that. I don't think I want to either." I was again struck by this combination of narcissistic contempt and schizoid loneliness in which Tony felt powerless and apart but also greater than his objects.

In the dozen visits I had with Tony before he abruptly terminated, he continued to present this sad and angry mixture of feelings that were administrated by this robot persona. Tony was a skinny, awkward looking man with a bad haircut and very thick glasses. Both of his eyes were "lazy," so neither one ever focused on me as we spoke. So, I never really knew if he was looking at me, and I never really knew which eye to be looking at when I spoke to him. This gave me a generally disinterested feeling on one hand and a sinister, creepy feeling at the same time. It made me feel like I was being scrutinized and under a microscope, trying hard to figure out how to be with him at any given moment. I felt like I was with a crazy scientist that was about to do something to me, but I also felt I needed to handle him in an extra careful and attentive manner since he seemed so fragile and alien. So, I felt strange and on edge but also bored, distant, and disengaged.

In her paper on working through the countertransference, Pick (1985) speaks to this when she says we are frequently disturbed and left anxious by the patient's transference projections and then we must find a way to contain this anxiety and offer an interpretation. The best, in-the-moment, mutative interpretation is usually one that we wish to avoid and that often scares us, but is hopefully most on target and most useful to the patient. So, I had to find a way to contain my disinterest, caution, and sense of being scrutinized in order to construct an interpretation that dealt with some of these projections.

Therefore, I interpreted that he was uninterested in being in treatment but also very anxious and feeling scrutinized by me. I added that he might be angry to feel stuck in such a place, having to see me in order to save his marriage and feeling in between his wife and me without much choice in the matter. Tony said, "I don't want to be here, but I thought you were supposed to tell me what to do so I can be more communicative with my wife." Here, he answered in not only a very concrete, stony manner but also in what felt to be an aggressive manner in which he suddenly put me in the position of his employee. I should hurry up and do my job so he can get on with better things. So, I asked him if he was angry and only wanting me to tell him what to do rather than actually giving himself a chance to learn about himself and what he wants. I wondered if he was curious about what he wanted rather than what I want or what his wife wants. He said, "I never think much about what I want. I never have. I never thought that was a choice."

The way he said this I felt he was directing us to his past. So, I asked him to tell me a bit about his family experiences. Afterwards, I understood some of what was taking place in the transference. I didn't take what he said as a perfect record of actual history, but more his own personal and now-distorted-by-time-and-phantasy record that he chose to relate to me at that moment in a particular way to me. Over the several sessions that he related his history, I found him to be more animated than ever before. This made me think he was truly still living in the grips of it and reluctant to step very far away from it into the wider world, as if today was more confusing and intimidating than the past and less in his control. This was the paranoid-schizoid aspect of it (Klein 1946) in which persecutory chaos was preferable to the lack of predictability and the complete loss of love that he envisioned if he were to be more himself and relate instead of hide. I thought he was also reluctant to let go of this paranoid security because he would have to face and accept the loss of what never was, the acceptance that what he hoped for never was and never will be. The pain of the past and the frightening uncertainty of the future combined with the accompanying mourning and grief of the depressive position (Klein 1935, 1940) to become an intolerable threat and unacceptable risk. I made these interpretations. Tony agreed, and after a moment he said friends have often told him to "chill out and relax and just talk about stuff," but he "can't and doesn't know how to." I said that perhaps it was because of the reasons I had just brought up. He said, "It might be." This seemed genuine, as genuine and vulnerable as Tony could be, and only a tad withholding or combative. The door seemed to open, even if just for a moment.

Tony's past was a story of ongoing abuse and constant anxiety. He told me that his father had been in the military and was always away during the day and often on the weekends. His mother was demanding, controlling, and prone to violence if Tony made her unhappy in any way. He said, "She would beat me if I didn't follow all her orders and often she would beat me for no reason at all. I could never get it right. I found the best approach to lay low and say and do nothing. But, ultimately that didn't work either. I had my face slapped so many times I can't count. She would yell at me all the time." Tony told me, "Life was hard because when I was home she was yelling at me or hitting me and at school I was the one everyone picked on. I had a speech impediment, thick glasses, and really bad acne. I got beat on and picked on all the time."

I asked him what his father did about all this, noticing Tony left him out of the picture. Tony said his father was usually at work, and when he was home, his mother was never violent. So, there was this secret violent life he had with mother and a pretend normalcy when father was home. Tony told me this all changed when Tony was about ten or twelve years old. The family was driving along, and when Tony did something his mother didn't approve of, she reached into the back seat and started to beat on him and scream at him. His father immediately stopped her and told her to never do that again, in no uncertain terms.

Tony said, "She never hit me again, but I was still always on the lookout." Here, I recalled my initial countertransference impression of him always being on guard against the bad object, so much so that he saw everything in that light. He relates to me and the world as a simplistic bad object to avoid, defend against, and feel superior to. When confronted with the reality of a much more complex and fair object, he does not know what to do. I interpreted that he cannot envision himself in a more complex, multilayered manner giving to the other as he receives from the other. Instead, he keeps himself in the box of mechanical lists and agendas free from dangerous emotion. I suggested that his wife may want him to be less in control, much like his friends tell him to "just relax." Tony agreed but said he didn't know how and "it isn't that easy to just suddenly become that." I said, "You heard me as telling you to hurry up and just turn the switch. You also have told me you are waiting for me to tell you the magic formula of how to turn the switch. I think you are angry when you realize how alone and stuck you feel." Tony said "yes" in a way that was true and open, but then quickly gone. It was a breath of fresh air before we suddenly hit the wall and were enveloped in the quicksand again.

Frequently, I felt Tony came in to the session and put me on the spot, saying, "What do we do now?" I felt this was a very precarious projective identification process in which he initially presented himself to me as a malleable piece of clay, ready to follow my orders, much like he must have tried to be with mother. But, very quickly, I felt on the spot to perform and deliver, under the sharp and critical eye of Tony and his concrete demands for "guidelines, advice, and techniques." So, I felt like he may have under the threat of mother's rigid threats, and he was now her and I was now him. I did my best to not get off balance in the countertransference and act out any of these feelings or thoughts. I tried to contain, understand, and work through my initial feeling of intimidation, anxiety, frustration, and resentment.

I interpreted that Tony was asking for a mechanical remedy to a problem of the heart. He replied, "I see everything that way. I want to put everything into that perspective because I can't imagine there being any other perspective." I interpreted that this lack of a "we" in his mind and heart was due to how uncertain and not in his control it felt, so he reduced it to a more manageable tool box, separating and neutralizing everything with more of a controlled "him" and "me" instead of a more uncertain or threatening "us." But, this defensive move simply left him trapped inside of the tool box, an alien who feels lost and alone in the world outside of that box.

We seemed to be making some progress or movement out of that box or at least we were able to explore the nature of that box a bit and see how and why he felt so completely confined yet comfortable in it. Unfortunately, Tony quit right about there. I received an eerie message on my answering machine that made me feel very creepy, as if a robot had called me. The message was delivered in an extremely monotone, emotionless machine tone: "Hello. My name is Tony. I am a patient of yours. You have seen me before. I have an appointment on Thursday. I will not be there. Good-bye." This was said in a halting, mechanical manner, and it was clear he felt I did not remember him and I would not know who he was if he didn't fully identify himself. I believe that through projective identification, Tony so split himself off from human contact to such an extreme that he was convinced I would never know him and he would never be able to connect with me. He felt like an alien who had to identify himself and remind me who he was. He would not allow himself into my mind or let me into his. So, to him we were both locked boxes wandering around without any mutual contact or any meaning or value for each other.

I called him back, and when he answered, the experience of being with a robot continued. I asked him what was going on, that his message was unclear. He said he "wasn't going to be at the appointment" and then he fell silent. I asked why, noting my frustration, irritation, and sense of being controlled or teased with his vague sentence and then the silence. Tony said he didn't see the use of coming in. I had to ask, "For this session or at all?," knowing full well he meant he was terminating but not wanting to engage with me about it. He said, "For any more" and then was silent for what seemed forever.

I said, now trying to address the transference, "Why are you seeing us as useless," using my countertransference feeling of being thrown away without much thought. Tony told me, "My wife has decided she wants to end the marriage. I came to see you to learn how to be different so she would stay. Now she has decided to go." Noting his robot-like lack of emotion over something so terrible, I said, "That is terrible. You must feel very bad." After a long silence, he said with anger in his voice, "Yes. I feel bad. What do you think?" Then, after another long period of silence, I said, "This must make you feel very unhappy. You tried to do what she wanted and she still doesn't want to be with you. You must be upset." After more silence, Tony said, in an emotionally laden moment, "I am really upset. I don't know what I am going to do. She said we could try couples therapy one more time, but she also said she doesn't think it will work and she is ready to file divorce papers."

I replied, "So, this might be a good time to have a place to talk and figure this out. Would you like to go ahead and meet next time?" Tony said, back to his stonily cold self, "No. I don't see the point. If she is leaving me, why would I keep going? I was coming to see you so she wouldn't leave me. I never got anything out of it anyway." This last comment was said with bitter hatred. Then, he fell silent again. I finally asked him what he was thinking and he said, "Nothing." Then, there was silence that went on and on. The unspoken and loud message was "I won't give to you. You will have to ask or beg." I asked Tony why he was being so withholding and why he seemed to be so angry with me. He told me, "You were supposed to tell me what to do and how to talk with her so she would be happier with me. You never gave me any advice or guidelines. And, you always asked for your money at the start of each session. It seemed like you cared more about money than anything else."

His comment about the money was one I have dealt with before with certain borderline and narcissistic patients who have issues around giving and feeling taken from. I tell everyone at the first session a few basic guidelines. One is about free association and the transference. One is about paying at the beginning of the session so we will not have to stop before the end of the session, while in the middle of something important, to have to write a check. However, some patients, like Tony, quickly fit my request for payment into their arsenal concerning phantasies of persecution and lack of understanding.

Then, I am forced into the position of proving my positive motivations and my genuine caring.

Tony's second comment about guidelines and advice was one he had raised before, and I had interpreted that he wanted me to take over like a good father who shows him how to be and helps Tony navigate his angry, rejecting mother/wife. I repeated this interpretation while consciously holding back and containing my irritation with his provocative style. He had no reply for a very long minute or two. I had to be the one to talk again and I said, "Would you like to come in and talk this Thursday?" He said, "No" and then fell silent again. Upon reflection, I believe he truly wanted to continue talking with me either on the phone or in person but could not bring himself to admit it or share it, as if it was a humiliation or a dangerous move. I was too caught up in my own feelings of frustration and helplessness to make that interpretation. Instead, I ended up telling him he was free to call me at any time and that I hoped he would change his mind and return. He never did call back.

In reflecting on this brief and difficult clinical encounter, I am impressed by the depth to which Tony refused to acknowledge any internal life, except for the occasional whisper of suffering he let out before slamming the door shut again. He would not allow any evidence of his own needs, opinions, or desire. In fact, instead of reaching for life and building on himself and his inner urges for satisfaction and gratification, he instead withdrew from life, withheld himself from others, and attacked the idea of a self and an object who could comfortably relate with each other. He simply tried to stave off the punishment of the other by pretending to not want anything to do with the world or with growth and relating. In fact, he held contempt for them. This made sense given his past experiences of neglect, disappointment, persecution, and betrayal by his early objects.

Segal (1993a) notes that birth confronts us all with the experience of need and dependence, which we react to in two possible ways. One can seek satisfaction for those needs which is life promoting (the life instinct) and creates opportunity to love and to be loved. Or, one can seek to deny, destroy, and distance from those needs and anything that may represent those needs (the death instinct). With patients such as Tony, we must painfully accept that the workings of the death instinct, as Segal describes them, may at this point in the life of the patient, be so entrenched that the unconscious phantasies of a bad self and/or a bad object will be forced onto the transference in such a way that we may simply not be able to help counter it in any significant manner. In other words, technically, the degree to which the death instinct is the foundation of the patient's defensive phantasy experience defines the analyst's ability to make sufficient analytic contact with the patient to help them slowly find hope and a reason to begin embracing life and themselves as a viable force in life.

Klein (1975) spoke of the relationship between envy and the death instinct. Normally, this translates to the patient's desire to destroy or neutralize what the object has that seems to be unavailable or withheld from the self. This was part of what made Tony have contempt for others who had the ability to "just make small talk." But he also was envious of the part of himself that on occasion dared to think and feel. During a few of his sessions, we spoke of how sometimes he would daydream and that in these daydreams he indeed had his own opinions about certain things. But, for the most part, he "saw that kind of thinking as useless and boring. It doesn't accomplish anything. What good is it for? And, it is only asking for conflict." So, Tony "stuck with whatever needed to be done next and didn't bother with feelings or thinking." He attacked his own sense of spontaneous thought and feeling with mechanical lists, logic, and agendas. I interpreted this to be both a way to stay out of trouble and conflict but also an attack on his own creativity and desire to think outside the box that he usually confines himself in.

Grotstein (2000) has noted the reparative function of hate. He describes how the death instinct has a primitive method of eliminating the bad object that stands in the way of life and love. I agree with this extension of Klein's concept, but for some patents like Tony, there is an added wrinkle. Because of the intense over-reliance on projective identification, a terrible pathological cycle is created in which the bad object is felt to be still approaching, over and over, so there needs to be still more hatred and aggression to ward it off. So, there is an eternal death instinct sentinel who always stands guard against the bad object, but in doing so, by always being at war, there is never a chance to realize that there may be no need for this constant vigilance. Peace may already exist, but the ego is still in the trenches, preparing for another battle.

CASE MATERIAL

Sue was a very difficult person struggling with very disturbing feelings and a sense of both superiority and helplessness. Her case was very similar to that of Tony. I only met with Sue for eight months before she terminated, telling me she "felt you never provided any help. You just left me out there without any map or any direction. I feel better anyway now and see no reason to continue." Sue did find some containment by working with me and found some relief from her chronic anxiety, but she left seeing me as unwilling and unable to give her this relief, thus validating her view of the selfish, cruel, and withholding nature of her objects.

I believe Sue is part of a group of borderline, narcissistic, psychotic, and primitive psychic retreat patients with whom we do our best to help but often run ashore after a very choppy trip though their stormy internal seas. When Sue left treatment, she never mentioned the money she owed or the possibility of meeting another time to discuss some of her concerns and see if we could find a solution. It was over and that was that. This lack of hope and negotiation is typical in the treatment of such patients. Their desire to give or receive is so tainted by the phantasy of demand or betrayal that love and hate become fused and confused to the point that attachment seems doomed to fail or sure to shift from something trustworthy to something dangerous.

Sue demonstrated Klein's concept of the total transference (1952) which Joseph (1985) has elaborated on and expanded into a vital center point for Kleinian technique. When Sue came to see me, it was for help with feeling extremely depressed over a series of recent changes in her life, including a job change, a move after her house burnt down, a death of a cousin she looked up to, and sudden worsening in her chronic intestinal condition.

About six years prior to her analytic treatment, Sue had developed a severe intestinal problem which made for intense stomach pain at any given time. She took prescription narcotics for the condition and had been hospitalized many times when the pain became overwhelming. She also stayed in bed when she felt too bad and would go to bed early in the day if the pain came on too strong. Sue was also over 100 pounds overweight, but was reluctant to discuss her use of food as a psychological issue.

Like in the case of Tony, Sue grew up in a family dominated by her volatile mother, who was an alcoholic and prone to violence. She beat Sue often, and Sue said she could "never tell when it was coming, but it was always terrifying." At the same time, she said she felt she knew "how to manipulate mother and please her so as to keep out of her way most of the time." Apparently, her father was helpless to protect the children and stayed out of the picture most of the time, leaving Sue and her sister to the wrath of their unpredictable mother. Interestingly, her father had a chronic back problem that left him in a wheelchair, kept him from working, and prevented him from leading a full productive life. His sickness and the help he constantly needed was a major part of what defined Sue's relationship with him. As an adult, Sue married a blind man, and their relationship was certainly shaped and impacted by his blindness and the special needs he had. So, chronic illness and physical problems that could not be controlled or cured was a theme in her life.

During the first few months of her analytic treatment, Sue used logic and cognitive control to manage our time together. By this, I mean she talked about the facts and details of things in a very superior "I know all the facts and have complete understanding about this" way that left out any emotional experience and immediately made her the one in charge. Sue was a very smart person and could indeed talk circles around any subject, but at the same time she used this intellectual approach to always avoid touching on any emotional exchange. When I interpreted this way of operating in the transference, she quickly put me in my place by asking, "So, what do you want me to do instead? I don't feel anything besides what I am talking about." Here, Sue demonstrated a variation on the theme Joseph (2000) has noted about patients who can act in a very compliant manner, but Sue's compliant approach was mixed with this rule of logic and the superiority of intelligence over emotionality. Here, I came to feel the total transference situation was suddenly taking shape and we were within a rapidly escalating situation in which Sue had no access to her feelings and I was positioned as the person with knowledge of emotions and how to express them. This was a difficult standoff in which she always won, leaving me feeling frustrated, confused, and somewhat belittled.

After a few more months, Sue began to exhibit another more intense and complex transference profile. She started coming in feeling much more anxious and depressed. She would cry the entire session and not know why. She told me, "I feel blackness all around me. I feels like something is coming for me and I don't know what it is or what to do!" She would begin sobbing and wailing and asking me, "What do I do???" and "What is it? I can't tell what it is! It just feels so overwhelming but I don't know what it is!" There was a tremendous demand to know and control, and the lack of control and not knowing seemed to be what left her in a panic, but the demand created more panic.

At some point, I interpreted that this unknown "presence that was coming at her" was the fear of her unpredictable mother coming at her and she wanted me to intervene. She replied with logic and rejecting demand, "So what do I do about that?!" I found myself with the countertransference feeling of being with a wild, writhing, and stomping animal that could only be handled with a dart gun full of tranquilizers. I wanted to tell her to just relax and we will make it through somehow. So, I interpreted, "You are overwhelmed and feel like you're about to be attacked. We must just make our way through it by talking about it and slowly understanding what it might be. But, we may not know for awhile. That is what seems to feel the worst, the not knowing."

Sue would just continue crying loudly and almost screaming, "It is awful. It is out there, but I can't tell what it is. I feel so scared. I can't take it anymore. What do I do???" So, in the countertransference, at first I felt we were both helpless and desperate. This alternated with feeling that she was being demanding and angry and I was being withholding and uncaring. So, I interpreted that she felt I was withholding and that she was upset with me for not immediately telling her exactly what was happening with her feelings and exactly what to do about it.

In a very concrete way, Sue said, "You got that right!" I also interpreted that she was making herself anxious by always needing to know exactly what was happening with her mind and heart before she even had a chance to explore it and gradually find out. She had to have it spelled out immediately and then eradicated with logic and knowledge as soon as possible. Again, she agreed in a very factual manner. This desire to know all and have everything and everyone controlled by her knowledge about them set up a vicious and fragile state of mind for Sue. Through projective identification, she set in motion a relational situation in which she was more and more out of control, feeling caught in a net of unknown and terrible feelings and desperately demanding I clue her in on what it was and what to do about it. So, I was seen as more and more useless, withholding, and uncaring, and she felt more and more overwhelmed, scared, and betrayed.

At one session, Sue was late in arriving and she then talked at length about how much she "felt off balance" and "odd and not sure where her footing was, like she was off balance and not sure where she would land." Again, she said this at great length but without any details or specific focus, just a general anxious state about something that seemed ominous and undefined. I tried to help her explore this and help her link it to any feelings or associations. She was able to tell me she felt she "was feeling scared of being in trouble," but she couldn't imagine why she felt that way and what it would possibly be related to.

I interpreted that she might be worried that I was angry with her for being late, that perhaps she was worried about how I might react and therefore she might be feeling afraid. In a dramatic mix of logic and intense affective phantasy, Sue replied, "You would never be violent with me like my mother was, so I don't think you are angry with me." In other words, she fused the idea of anger and violence and was not able to see me as being irritated with her without the added fear of violence. I think this created a severe confusion in her mind in which she probably did fear that I was angry with her for being late but then faced either having me be a violent, out-of-control mother or a neutralized, flat object that had no impact on her, negative or positive.

So, by sticking with this neutralized method of coping, Sue was safe but adrift and alone. When I made these interpretations, she told me she hoped I would show her how to deal with things and point out what these strange unknown scary feelings were, but she didn't picture that I would ever have any emotional impact on her. So, I was a useless object to her suffering or I became the source of her suffering. And, when I asked her to explore some of these traumatic memories, she used the same attempt at control through logic and told me she "knew how to deal with mother, knew how to handle her."

Unfortunately, this pathological psychic retreat (Steiner 1990) broke down and did not provide much of a respite from the ravages of both paranoid and depressive fears, leaving Sue to feel helpless against the worst of her mind's conflicts (Waska 2010c). Therefore, she was left in the projective identification-based cycle of first fearing an attacking object, then wanting an object that would help and soothe her, and then finally refusing help, claiming supreme autonomy and control, and thereby feeling abandoned and cruelly left to suffer. This transference grew and solidified over time until Sue terminated, citing how she both felt "better and more in charge of things" and "not helped or guided in any way." In some ways, she deposited those feelings of unknown panic into me as when she terminated, I was left feeling, "What was that? What was that strange thing that swooped in to my office and then swooped out? What was that!?"

In conclusion, the modern psychoanalytic practitioner sees a great deal of troubled people who are so entrenched in various paranoid and depressive phantasies that they can barely tolerate these conflicts, let alone work on them for any period of time before retreating back into their well-known methods of hiding, defending, and blurring their internal pain. So, we meet for what is often a very short chaotic excursion into the wilderness of their mind before they abruptly terminate. At best, we help these patients to contain and sometimes work out a modest portion of internal chaos before they lurch back down the road. Perhaps this is a valuable service and needs to be respected as part of what true psychoanalysis is about. It does tax our countertransference ideal of what we should be doing in the field according to our training models. But, we remain true psychoanalysts if we attempt to stay on course with Klein's views of working in the transference (Spillius 1996). The contemporary Kleinian method and my approach of analytic contact are best summarized by the technical principles of making mutative interpretations in the here-and-now moment of the total transference situation, while trying to be aware of and utilize the constant pull to settle into various enactments brought upon us by complex cycles of projective identification, typical to most patients' transference dynamics.

7

The Object Relational Struggles of Libidinal and Destructive Narcissists

There are some patients who come in to see us to assure themselves and others that they are without a mark, that they do their best to care for their objects, and that any trouble or conflict with the object is something they are innocent of. These are usually high-functioning narcissistic individuals who cannot bear to take responsibility for their actions, but still feel dangerously close to being exposed for being the cause of hurt and corruption and therefore open to attack. They exist in a psychological realm of both paranoid and depressive phantasy, presenting both primitive guilt and a narcissistic stance that is only partially open to change.

They use us and the analytic setting to rebuild the broken object and do so as if they should be awarded for the effort instead of called out as the one who did the injuring. These patients seem to always live in distance from their objects, keeping a superior and defensive distance between them and the reality of real objects that they are impacting. So, rather than face that they are with unsatisfying, injured, or murdered objects, they dress them up with tales of "we are still friends even after the divorce," "we certainly never have any hard feelings," "you are my therapist, why would I ever have any negative feelings towards you?" This type of idealized, no conflict/all love world is so hardened and defended in some patients that it becomes a manic, destructive, "stab you in the back while smiling in your face" type of persona. Other times, it is less lethal but still carries a certain dishonest approach in which one thinks, "This is too good to be true. They are too nice to be real." There can be a suspicious, mistrusting countertransference reaction in which one feels eerily on guard for a fraudulent act, a bait and switch of some sort. A very disguised and denied destructive, criminal, or manipulative style can raise countertransference red flags, leaving the analyst worried about what the patient may do to them or what kind of monster lurks beneath the surface.

Another countertransference reaction is activated by the intense nature of the projective identification process encountered with such individuals. They lack the confidence to be direct, expressive, or forthcoming and instead have to act in subtle and roundabout ways. Over and over, they seem to end up being lead by the object. They try and please the object, only to feel resentful or unhappy and then resort to more passive-aggressive maneuvers. There are frequent oedipal triangles which leave them feeling caught between two stronger objects that strangulate their own free will. In these situations, the patient often feels panicked to please both objects and sacrificing their own needs in the process. Thus, there is a guilt-ridden depressive need to please and never cause harm to the object combined with a more paranoid-schizoid narcissistic desire to own, control, and omnipotentily deny any responsibility. A weak and passive person who is unable to handle conflict alternates with an aggressive, cold, and calculating person ready to lie to save their image and have their way. This is one type of destructive defensive system (Segal 1972) or pathological organization (Steiner 1987) in which the ego is structured around defending against the constant threat of both paranoid and depressive conflicts without any available respite due to intense cycles of projective identification.

CASE MATERIAL

Originally, Joe came to see me after feeling very anxious about telling his wife that he felt they "were incompatible." He told me he wanted to "make sure he handled it with respect and care because he loved his wife and wanted to let her down easy and not hurt her feelings." He said he needed help in coming to terms with how to decide if separation or divorce was the best thing for the family. He said, "Sadly, divorce might be the healthiest choice for all involved."

I felt like all this was said in an effort to sound kind, loving, and concerned about the other, but in fact Joe seemed fake and just trying to appear supportive and loving. He was too good to be true. This countertransference feeling was combined with the strange notion that he was gay but perhaps trying to hide it from himself and others. Over the course of several months, I realized that this observation was probably the result of his severe split between what he said and what he felt being embodied in the effeminate and posed manner he bodily presented himself. It was difficult for Joe to be his own man and instead he had found a way to blend in with his wife and mistress, pleasing them through imitation, and I believe this came through in how he carried himself physically. He was in constant conflict and pulled by anxieties of love and hate as he found himself in the middle of these two women and he gradually took on much of their ways as a method of pleasing, avoiding conflict, and as a way to manipulate and control.

Joe embodied numerous contrary aspects of self and other and brought them to bear in the transference situation. Quickly, I felt he was being passively lead around by his girlfriend whom he had been having a one-year affair with. He finally acknowledged to himself how sick he was of trying to please his wife without feeling much reward in return. In discussing his relationship with his girlfriend, I interpreted he was looking to me to step in as a father who would tell him it was OK to stand up to the object and voice his own opinions, that it wouldn't hurt or destroy the object. Also, I interpreted he was looking to me for reassurance that he wouldn't face punishment or retaliation from the object if he voiced his differences. Here, I was interpreting the immediate here-and-now transference (Joseph 1989) which was at that particular juncture the more depressive, guilt-ridden side of Joe, passive and unsure of how to negotiate with his objects without hurting them or causing trouble.

However, I think his narcissistic rationalization was so strong that he went ahead and did as he pleased in a very camouflaged manner. Therefore, I chose to confront him and interpret his more paranoid aggressive stance. I said, "You are trying to make me see you as a polite guy who would never do anything wrong, yet you are having your way and pretending it is in the service of being nice. What you are telling me is one thing: you are trying to say you are a nice guy who just realized it would be better for you and your wife to separate and you want to help her through this difficult period and conduct yourself in the most respectful way possible. But, what you are actually doing is leaving your wife for another woman, a woman you have had a secret affair with for over a year now. So, we have to understand why things need to be so dressed up and non-direct."

I felt this was a helpful interpretation that indeed assisted Joe to begin looking at himself and his way of relating a bit closer. But, I was also aware of my own pushiness and desire for him to own his manipulation and to own up to trying to pull one over me and his wife. If he wanted to act sleazy, he should at least own up to it. So, here I think I was putting myself over him much like he already felt his objects were judging and prodding him. But, I was also reacting to a certain narcissistic grandiosity, coldness, and detachment that left me irritated, slightly scared, and manipulated. So, I think my interpretation was both accurate and helpful, but a bit of a countertransference enactment as well.

Over the course of our short time together, Joe presented many stories that all converged into this same transference profile in which he was reassuring me that everything and everyone was OK and happy and the "right thing" was being done. This was a manic and violent series of projective identification dynamics that was designed to keep Joe elevated as the object's honest and sincere protector and "good guy." But, it also served to disguise the more manipulative and selfish aspects of his desires and his dishonest and not so "good guy" ways. Given the nature and intensity of my countertransference, I assumed he was desperately and calculatingly depositing his guilt and his aggression into me. At the same time, the other more dependent and passive transference seemed to be part of an effort to communicate his anxieties around rejection and punishment to me. With libidinal narcissists, this combination of evacuative and communicative projective identification is common.

Overall, I believe Joe's unconscious mission in treatment was to use me as a dump site for these ugly and unwanted pieces of himself and then to move on to his undisturbed narcissistic state of being the superior "good guy." I think he would have left treatment even sooner had I not interrupted this dump site mentality by continuously interpreting and confronting him about his deeper motives.

At the same time, he was struggling with a sense of wondering where his objects were and trying to not impact anyone with his needs or opinions especially if they might cause conflict. This was where he was able and willing to communicate more openly and use projective identification in a healthier manner as opposed to aggressive evacuation and omnipotent control. So, I also interpreted those transference dynamics which seemed to help him temporarily examine himself and learn a bit, but he quickly used that knowledge in the service of having things go his way, making them conflict-free so he could still be the "good guy."

Within the first couple of visits with Joe, I learned that after a year into his seven-year marriage, Joe felt he did not love his wife. He never tried to talk to his wife about it. Indeed, he said he "never completely noticed it, just went about my business." He said he simply "tried to go with the flow, and when he noticed the lack of love, he hoped that things would just get better somehow." Here, I felt he was describing his very passive, almost masochistic style of relating in which he had no say and did not want to disturb the object with his needs or differences. Joe said he would have left his wife, but when they had their first child, he "tried to give it a chance." But, when they had their child, he also felt "the marriage was all for show. I had zero feelings for her, but I didn't really realize it." When he said he didn't realize it, I thought he was describing how he denied his differences but also attacked his needs and beat them into submission.

I interpreted that perhaps he didn't allow himself to realize it as it would have rocked the boat and caused conflict. Here, I was interpreting the more depressive side of Joe's conflicts and his depressive fear for his object and of his objects. Joe agreed and said he "has never liked conflict and has never said anything in his life to stir things up." Here again, I felt he was showing me a strong depressive fear of creating turmoil with his objects, protecting them from what felt like an aggressive, destructive set of needs, desires, or reactions. His narcissistic control and deception left the object broken and bleeding, so Joe had to find a way to deny it or be extra nice and respectful to magically save and heal them. This primitive narcissistic guilt mixed with a more ominous paranoid greed and envy that left him controlling things with a veiled aggressive strategy and then feeling guilt and having to pick up the pieces with a smile.

As mentioned earlier, Joe had begun an affair with his wife's best friend a year before coming to see me. After a year of going behind his wife's back, Joe worried about what would happen if he were to spend more time with his girlfriend and what would happen if his wife found out. I interpreted that he seemed torn between getting into trouble, hurting others, and not able to have it his way anymore. Here, I interpreted the combined conflict at that moment because the pathological splitting, the intense projective identification, and the resulting overlap and blur of depressive and paranoid urges he so often operated within had momentarily decreased, leaving him a bit more responsive and reflective. Joe responded by telling me he wanted to have a "full relationship with this new woman that he loved but felt unsure how his wife would react. He said his girlfriend "had told him he had to wait and not create a soap opera." Joe said this like he was a dog on a leash, not wanting to disobey but angry to be so restrained.

I interpreted that Joe felt like a little man stuck between these two powerful women. He was trying hard to please both, not hurt both, but ending up feeling controlled by both and not ever getting his way. So, he had to manipulate everyone and look like the "good guy" who always did the right thing but really was secretly maneuvering to get his way. Joe basically agreed with my comments but in a very concrete manner, with no reflection or questioning of his own. He said, "So? What is strange about that?" Here, I felt we were switching from the more passive, depressive, and masochistic side of Joe to the more narcissistic and aggressive side. The primitive guilt and anxiety was unbearable, so he summoned the paranoid-schizoid troops to rally to his defense.

In coming to see me, Joe described his goal to be the "healthy and thoughtful resolution to the problem so that all parties would have their needs met in a respectful manner." This type of fluffy and controlling camouflage was Joe's main method of relating to me. Over the course of several sessions, it became clear that he did not want to own the feelings, responsibilities, or consequences associated with his decision to have an affair and to now file for divorce. He wanted me and others to see him as "doing the right thing in a caring and respectful manner."

In the countertransference, I felt he was exhibiting a shallow, controlling, and naïve way of being with his objects. At the same time, it appeared that he felt very passive and stuck between bigger and more fragile objects that he needed or depended on.

So, I found myself interpreting that Joe was trying to make me see him in a nice light, as trying to do the right thing, in order to hide a more selfish and assertive motive that he seemed to feel guilty about and afraid of the turmoil it might cause. So, here I was interpreting a type of libidinal narcissism, similar to what Rosenfeld (1987) spoke of. I used the word guilty, but to myself I was struck by how he seemed to have this radical split, so characteristic of narcissism. On one hand, a part of himself did feel guilty seeking out a new relationship and wanting love and pleasure because he could hurt everyone's feelings and he could get caught and get into conflict, which he dearly avoided. This was all part of a more primitive depressive conflict.

On the other hand, Joe seemed to simply be trying to get away with having his way without getting caught and looking bad. In fact, he was trying to convince me that he was a really good-hearted fellow instead of a manipulative con artist. So, while I interpreted the more neurotic, passive, and guilt-ridden transference state, I also confronted the more manipulative, malignant narcissistic transference by telling him, "You are trying to tell me the story in a way that makes you look like you only have everyone else's needs in mind. But, in fact, you seem to be manipulating me and others by not acknowledging you have been fed up for years, unsatisfied, in your marriage, been cheating on your wife for over a year, and now want a divorce so you can go be with your girlfriend." This interpretation was in line with Rosenfeld (1987) and other leading Kleinians' ideas regarding the nature of destructive narcissism.

Joe's denial-based, sleight-of-hand approach invited me to be the one who set him straight and asked him to stop pulling the wool over our eyes. On one hand, I felt I had to pull the lid off his shady, narcissistic manner of being with others. Then, I would feel compelled to "make" him "see" that he was manipulating and hurting others by lying. On the other hand, I felt like I was giving voice to more aggressive, expressive needs he usually felt too passive or fearful to voice and then felt trapped by his obligations to be nice and avoid conflict. So, even in dealing with his more destructive controlling side, I felt there was an element of communication, via projective identification, in which he invited me to be a parental figure, setting him straight. So, my confrontive and interpretive blend of technique seemed to serve not only as an unintentional countertransference enactment release, but also as a response to Joe's unconscious request for a direct, honest parental object who could tolerate conflict, have opinions, show disagreement and challenge, and voice differences. This is not to say I was trying to give him advice, but to make confrontive interpretations that did not avoid potential harm to the object when it was felt to be in the interest of the patient's growth. In other words, when I confronted him, I was in essence answering his unconscious projective identification based-question: "Is it OK to be selfish by honestly telling the other what I feel, think, and need even if it may rub them the wrong way? Is it OK to be direct and open even if it means creating tension and conflict?" Also, confrontation can help the patient, especially the narcissistic patient, to understand the normal splitting of what is right and wrong, good and bad. A fundamental aspect of narcissistic functioning is the breakdown of healthy splitting so that there is no clear definition of bad and good, only distorted blurs of idealized perfection and nothing or perfect union and bloody conflict.

A significant aspect of Joe's transference seemed to be his resistance to having to face the depressive level injury and impact he had on his objects. He wanted more from the object than he already had but was reluctant to express it openly. But, this desire made him feel ruthless and harmful. Indeed, he seemed to do whatever he could to deny the damage he did, past and present, to his objects. In this way, he was constantly avoiding the graveyard of his deeds, celebrating happiness and turning away from grief, loss, and painful separation. This is in line with what Kernberg (2009) states to be a part of the death instinct in which patients unconsciously destroy time and the events that have occurred with significant objects as well as the important feelings attached to those objects.

While Kernberg and others (Segal 1993a) note these destructive actions in more severely disturbed patients, I believe we can witness the same type of phenomenon in patients like Joe, who live within a combination of paranoid narcissism and depressive, masochistic loss. This combination can create the vulnerable/shut-off, concerned/callous, and actively manipulating/passively controlling profile Joe presented. This creates a confusing clinical situation in which the patient is on one hand wanting us to help them save or heal their objects from hurt, constantly wanting us to validate their efforts at pleasing and feeding their objects (Rey 1988). On the other hand, these same patients use us to shore up their eroding narcissistic rationalizations and sense of righteousness so as not to feel weak and dependent.

When I explored Joe's deeper motives for his cold and manipulative ways by both confronting him and interpreting his conflicts, several things occurred. Through projective identification, he was asking me to be the direct and honest voice of what was really going on. He wanted to protest to his internal objects and tell them off and make them properly care for him, but he was unable to take this task on, so he projected into me. He could never feel safe enough or strong enough to put things so directly. So, I think my confrontive interpretations were indirectly helpful to this more depressive sense of helplessness and fear. At the same time, I was meeting his more destructive narcissistic side face on and asking him to consider and own that more aggressive and manipulative side for a moment.

However, the essence of Joe's entire brief treatment seemed to be his using me to regain his narcissistic stance, and my interpretations only slowed this inevitable process down a bit. He wanted help with being able to stand up and tell his wife he wanted a divorce, to tell his girlfriend to not try and run his life, and to make his own decisions for himself. He used me to gain ground in his normally passive and manipulated self-experience and turn towards this other more independent, manipulative side. So, rather than help him work through some of these conflicts and pathological splits, I was utilized as a first-aid kit to get back to his regular psychic equilibrium (Joseph 1989) or a psychological pit stop on the way back to his narcissistic sense of power and secret control.

Three weeks before Joe stopped coming to his analytic treatment, we were discussing his young child's reaction to him having moved out and filed for divorce. Joe told me he thought his son "was having a little trouble adjusting to his father's moving out, but all and all everything seemed just fine." Feeling like Joe was again painting a false and eerie happy face on everything, I asked for details. Joe told me, "They told me he was acting a little strange in school, and he has become more clingy than ever before. He is somewhat upset and fussy sometimes and asks about where I am. But, he has always been somewhat sensitive or emotional."

After listening to a few more details about his son's reactions, I interpreted that his son was upset, probably sad and angry to lose his father and see his parents splitting up. I proposed that Joe seemed uncomfortable acknowledging this because these "sensitive" feelings were too anxiety provoking so he had to eliminate them and see everything and everybody as doing fine and well. Joe replied, "My mother and father divorced when I was five years old. I remember one day my father was suddenly gone. That was it. They were not together anymore." I asked him how that felt. He said, "I remember having no feelings at the time about it. None at all. I was OK with it and had no problems. So, since my son is about the same age, I am surprised to see his reaction. I don't understand why he would have any problem with it."

Here, I felt the same dual set of countertransference feelings that had followed me throughout the treatment, matching Joe's dual set of transferences.

I thought that Joe was being cold and hollow in a way that felt strange and frightening. I wanted to shake him and tell him to have a heart, but I also felt very sorry for that little boy who had to hide from the trauma.

I interpreted, "You seem to have found a way to shut down your sorrow, anger, and fear from very early on, convincing yourself and now me that you were fine, even when you lost your parents as a family unit. But, the way you feel stuck under the thumb of your wife, your girlfriend, and then the both of them without any voice tells me you get worried about saying what you need. So, instead you have to smile on the outside and say it is all OK while feeling angry on the inside and trying to manipulate your way to what you want. You must feel really pulled in all directions by yourself and by others." This last piece was my interpretation of the results of his excessive use of projective identification.

Joe replied, "I don't like it when my girlfriend tells me what to do and what we will be doing next. I have been afraid of saying anything about what I need to either my wife or my girlfriend because I was afraid they would be angry or leave me. But, the last few times after seeing you, I was able to tell my girlfriend what I felt, and I also let her know that I would understand if she couldn't be with me afterwards. But, I had to stick to what I felt was right for me." Here, I felt he was being honest and had made some significant steps forward. He was able to speak more directly to the object without fear of hurting the object or being hurt by the object. Joe, for right now, had a new moment in which he did not have to outwardly comply and inwardly rebel.

Joe's treatment was brief and unsuccessful as far as his actual working through of underlying patterns and conflicts. However, my hope is that he was left with some degree of interest in reflecting on his internal patterns and perhaps occasionally questioning them.

My pattern of making fairly strong and direct confrontations that sometimes bordered on accusations were at times countertransference enactments of Joe's desire to tell off cold, narcissistic, or unavailable objects, perhaps mummified images of his separating parents. I think my interpretations were at times also enactments based on his projective identification need to be told, guided, and taught what to do and feel given permission to "go for it." He wanted permission to not be afraid of causing conflict or not having to always please others by waiting for their decisions and opinions.

Unfortunately, sometimes our therapeutic balance is unstable, and many times our interpretations are a blend of enactment and therapeutic accuracy. So, I think that along with the various interpretative enactments, I was able to make various interpretations that truly did help Joe take a modest and brief look at himself in a new way than before. This insight allowed for a small change in how he treated himself and others.

Joe suffered from both paranoid-schizoid level narcissistic entitlement and depressive level guilt and anxiety. These conflicts and phantasies led him to make massive efforts at avoiding any dependence on the object. Nor would he acknowledge any damage he inflicted on his objects or desire to replace his current object with a better object and the aggression that might entail. So, by pleasing others and being passive and avoiding conflict, Joe could simply be rewarded by fate for being a nice boy rather than someone whose needs or desires are different or even hurtful to some degree to the object. This more real sate of occasional friction would make him feel guilty or fearful of reprisal.

DISCUSSION
Feldman (in Steiner 2008) emphasizes how Herbert Rosenfeld advocated the gradual and careful examination of what the patient was projecting and instead of reacting or enacting, the analyst must slowly bring their understanding of the projections to the patient's attention. Rosenfeld discussed how critical it is to tolerate and slowly translate the projections and to trust that along with the aggressive, destructive aspects, these assaultive projections also serve some sort of communicative function. This was certainly the case with Joe. I struggled to not act out his projections and narcissistic manipulations long enough to try and grasp what might be there besides the outright aggressive desire to own and possess, eliminating differences no matter what. Eventually, I felt there were important aspects of Joe's internal relational struggle being communicated to me through the transference.

Feldman goes on to note that while timing is important, the analyst cannot fail to realize that the patient is in need of constant interpretation regardless of how forceful and attacking the resistance may be. I do think that patients who are more fragile and thin-skinned narcissists (Rosenfeld 1987) certainly can need ongoing interpretations to feel consistently fed by the object, and without this constant predictable flow of verbal feeding, the patient can have a sense of abandonment, deprivation, and attack. However, I think the same is true with more destructive forms of narcissism, the thick-skinned variety (Rosenfeld 1987). But, along with interpretations, the analyst needs to use interpretive confrontation to stand up to and hopefully break through some of the more rigid and omnipotent forms of transference often encountered. This is a way to temporarily slow down the psychotic distortion so often seen in the more narcissistic disorders in which the patient is inviting the analyst to join them in an intense sphere of denial, superiority, and control.

Feldman notes how Rosenfeld discovered that with more disturbed patients the analyst must demonstrate their capacity to survive the projective attacks by making sympathetic and containing interpretations. I would also argue that with some more masochistic or narcissistic patients, a more confrontive and direct method of interpreting may also help to break through their massive need for control and independence. In fact, I see these two methods of interpreting being mutually supportive and more potent when used side by side specifically when working with patients who tend to slide back and forth between paranoid and depressive functioning. When the patient sees that we are willing to understand them and to survive their attacks as well as stand up and represent a different way of living and relating, their level of paranoia and anxiety reduces. However, as Rosenfeld and Feldman note, this creates a sudden shift to dependence and ownership of one's actions that in turn creates an immediate flight into denial, avoidance, paranoia, and anxiety. So, there can be a slow going, one step forward and one or two back type of vicious cycle with such patients.

Ron Britton (in Steiner 2008) summarizes how Herbert Rosenfeld thought narcissistic disorders came out of the failure to reach successful splitting between good and bad in the paranoid-schizoid position. This could be brought about by both constructional factors as well as a parental failure in containing and holding. Such patients have an idealized aspect of themselves and an idealized image of an object, which, when challenged by the analyst, can be felt as a threat to this narcissistic bond of ideal to ideal. Therefore, I am advocating a combination of confrontation, in some situations, with empathic interpretations regarding the defensive nature of the destructive or aggressive attacks. I say "in some situations" because I think the more purely destructive narcissists, while still having aspects of libidinal narcissistic conflicts, are on one hand prone to provoking confrontations that are more blaming enactments than productive interpretations and cannot utilize the confrontations as much even when they are balanced with empathic interpretations. For those patients, containment and interpretation of the anger, paranoia, and anger with self and object are more clinically important.

Finally, Rosenfeld tried to make a distinction between libidinal narcissism, which was defensive, and destructive narcissism, which was based more on sheer envy, murderous intent, and the desire to create suffering and surrender. Modern Kleinians see the narcissistic patient as unable or unwilling to form or acknowledge a healthy working relationship with the analyst. Some remain aloof and distant, and others are very sterile and concrete in their transference, but both see the analyst as insignificant. The analyst is either a servant or a personal assistant, one who reassures and never challenges. Any experience of difference or challenge is either ignored, dismissed, attacked, or eliminated by terminating the relationship.

My clinical experience has been that the more libidinal narcissist exists within a torturous emotional zone between paranoid and depressive states of mind which allows the analyst to engage them in a brief and rocky reflection that can sometimes produce a more stable working relationship and other times results in a temporary pit stop in which the patient uses the analyst to regain their psychic equilibrium before terminating. This was the case with Joe. The more destructive narcissist is operating mostly within the paranoid-schizoid zone of experience and therefore will view most exploration by the analyst as persecutory and will react accordingly.

Rosenfeld (1987) thought that libidinal narcissistic patients will exhibit resentment, revenge, and withdrawal when challenged, but some will eventually allow for difference, reflection, and insight. They will sometimes allow change. This is in line with my own clinical approach of attempting to establish analytic contact (Waska 2007) with narcissistic patients. The use of combined confrontation and interpretation, addressing both offensive and defensive intent, will create the resentment and withdrawal Rosenfeld described, but will also create a vital opportunity or potential for working-through, insight, and change.

But, the destructive narcissist will react to the same approach with intense, but sometimes masked, envy, rage, and the desire to completely destroy or eliminate the analyst and his or her ideas. Hanna Segal and other Kleinians see narcissism as primarily destructive and equate it with the death instinct. Life-giving relationships and healthy self-love are both regarded as the enemy. Most patients have aspects of both libidinal and destructive narcissism in combination at differing levels often within a pathological organization (Steiner 1987) or destructive defensive systems (Segal 1972). In terms of origin, Britton (in Steiner 2008) thinks that libidinal narcissism usually is the result of poor parental containment and interpersonal communication and that destructive narcissism usually emerges from the infant's own hatred of the object. I agree with these ideas but also think both can easily fuel each other.

Riccardo Steiner (in Steiner 2008) notes the importance of slowing the analytic exploration process down so as to gradually make sense of the intense and disturbed splitting process so common with disturbed patients. By immersing himself within the fragmentation, the analyst is able to slowly understand and interpret the various pieces of the psychic puzzle before him and help the patient make sense of it. I (Waska 2006, 2007, 2010a) have written about this process as well and find it critical with borderline, narcissistic, and psychotic patients. Even though the overall clinical picture may remain fuzzy and uncertain, the most helpful clinical approach seems to be to take the close, here-and-now, moment-to-moment examination of the total transference (Joseph 1985) and use the complete countertransference (Waska 2010b) to slowly make sense of, contain, translate, and interpret the projective identification-based transference.

Pathological splitting and intense use of projective identification are two very common ways of relating and non-relating encountered with the more difficult patient. Rosenfeld and other Kleinians have discovered how there is a breakdown or failure in the normal or healthy development of splitting so essential for the gradual shift from paranoid to depressive functioning. Narcissistic patients typically resist healthy splitting as it takes away the complete and infallible idealization they depend on. Splitting creates the risk of failure, of difference, and of disappointment in self and object, so splitting is avoided, distorted, or perverted. Many of the borderline or narcissistic patients we struggle to help have suffered confusing and undermining childhood experiences with their primary objects. Therefore, it is useful to take this into account in building on understanding of how and why the patient is constructing the transference they do. Often, we may mistakenly replay some of those traumatic childhood patterns by making defensive interpretations that were too quick, too strong, or insensitive in response to the patient's aggressive or arrogant ways of relating. Only paying attention to the destructive aspects of narcissism is not helpful. One should always examine the communicative function of the patient's pathology as well.

At the same time, one should not turn away from analyzing the destructive aspects of the transference which are not always defensive in nature. Predatory motives can exist independently or side-by-side more traumatized and defensive motives. However, I think that it is essential to always be looking for what the underlying communication might be no matter how confusing or destructive it may seem.

Borderline and narcissistic patients, including those operating within fragile combinations of both depressive and paranoid pathology, can come to focus on the analyst and the analyst's mind as a threat, a source of judgment, or a lack of support. The narcissistic patient takes the best of the object, according to what fits his omnipotent phantasy, identifies with it, and withdraws into himself. Any undesirable aspects of the object are rejected, and unacceptable aspects of the self are ignored or projected.

Often, the analyst will be treated as a dump zone for all projected bad elements of self or object. The patient may idealize this situation and be surprised, offended, or threatened if the analyst challenges this use of the treatment setting as an emotional toilet or dump site. In fact, many narcissistic patients simply use the analyst and the therapeutic setting as a pit stop to discard unwanted aspects of self or other until they can feel better, stronger, and in command, and then they move on. They see the analyst as employed to fulfill this duty as an emotional toilet, personal assistant, or someone who should simply listen and agree with everything they say. Advice can only be in the patient's favor, never a challenge, never a difference to what the patient desires.

With Joe, he idealized my confrontations and interpretations as the right advice on how to stand up to his objects without having to feel responsible about hurting them. He was able to take some ownership of his actions when he did stand up and express himself to his wife and girlfriend, but he also used me as a conduit of parental permission and guidance. He also used me as a dump site for unwanted guilt, anxiety, and loss that he refused to own, tolerate, or bear. My confrontations brought these unwanted elements back into the fray, and he had to take a second look at some of them.

John Steiner (2008) writes about narcissism as a defense against separateness. The object is experienced as a part of the self or an extension of the self, and any differences or aspects of the analyst that do not fit into that ideal are shunned, ignored, or attacked. I think that after Joe used me for ideas that helped him and that fit with what he could tolerate, he shunned any expansion of thought past what he felt was a non-conflicted, happy ending to his current external problem.

Contemporary Kleinians see envy, separateness, and dependency as all part of the threat narcissistic patients defend against. Unbearable feelings of envy make it difficult to tolerate separateness. I think this type of envy includes phantasies of objects who are able to be successfully dependent as well as objects who do not seem to be in pain over not knowing, lack of control, and separateness. In other words, these patients see others having healthy experiences of separateness and dependency that they cannot find for themselves, so they become destructively envious and narcissistically independent in reaction.

Or, as in the case of Joe, he convinced himself and tried to convince me that his current object relational predicament was normal, fine, and OK. In that way, he could include himself in the rest of the crowd and be one of those who found ways to live and relate peacefully and happily. Therefore, Joe wasn't envious because he had what everyone else had. This phantasy of having what other's have is unique to the narcissistic patient who is both depressive and paranoid in character (the libidinal narcissist). The more destructive, paranoid narcissist is overwhelmed with envy and simply wants to destroy what he thinks others have.

In my own clinical work, I see loss as being a significant factor for narcissistic patients. Certainly, to be dependent brings about the potential of loss, and being separate can turn into loss. So, these states are always avoided, and the illusion of control over loss is maintained. For Joe, his sad story about his parents divorcing and him claiming to feel nothing spoke volumes about the way he has had to live a distant and separate life from the object, in control and safe, but alone and empty.

I find that the litmus test for many narcissistic patients is often simply asking if they are feeling loss as a result of the current crisis in their life. Inevitably, much as Joe did, they will answer with a stoic, cold, and omnipotent denial of having any problems in that area. Defiance, denial, and omnipotent rationalization are common responses. Herbert Rosenfeld (1987) thought direct and compassionate interpretations will successfully lead the narcissistic or borderline patient to experience his need for others and his lack of control and power over others and over himself. When this happens, the patient can feel very depressed, humiliated, or fragmented.

Even though it seems almost cruel to repeatedly expose the patient to these terrible feelings of shame, fear, and persecution, Rosenfeld argues that these conflicts and feelings must be faced, understood, and worked through if genuine object relationships are to ever be established and a real sense of self-love and acceptance of self regardless of faults is to blossom. This is in line with my own approach of analytic contact (Waska 2007) that sometimes includes interpretations which are confrontive but still aimed at helping the patient face their internal anxieties over loss, control, dependence, aggression, and separateness. Once out of their dark hiding place and into the clearing, they will feel exposed and vulnerable but also able to take a step towards something new, something less rigid and confining and more flexible and expansive. Forgiveness, acceptance, give and take, trust, and security are all potential rewards for this frightening risk to the controlled, frozen state of self and other so comfortable and familiar. Hopefully, we can introduce these patients to the idea that gratitude and love can bring together the life and death instincts instead of envy being a default weapon designed to eliminate all signs of life and difference. Among Kleinians, there is much useful clinical discussion about the death instinct as sometimes purely destructive and based on destroying the object out of envy as well as the need to be omnipotent. This theoretical and clinical stance is in parallel to the Kleinian idea of the death instinct as a way to eliminate any obstacles or threats to the good object and the good self. All these factors are often found in combination with our more difficult cases.

When the narcissistic patient makes a temporary and brief but genuine bond or psychological contact with others, he suddenly faces the realization that he is not supreme, not independent, and not able to be in complete control of himself or his object. He suddenly sees he cannot prevent pain to the object or pain from the object. He is within the depressive experience. Rosenfeld discusses how when libidinal narcissism is the major element in the patient's internal structure, contact with objects brings about a sense of loss, depression, anxiety, guilt, and uncertainty that then activates other more primitive or destructive defenses. When destructive narcissism is more the presenting element, contact with an object brings out anxiety, humiliation, and persecution which motivate strong attacks on the persecutory object and a move to immediately gain back a sense of independence, control, and superiority.

Herbert Rosenfeld (Rosenfeld 1987) was a pioneer in noticing the many different forms of projective identification and how some patients use the analyst as a method to expel unwanted aspects of self or internal objects. Other patients use projective identification as a communication device and desire a response and understanding from the analyst. Some of these ideas are similar to Bion's (1962b) regarding containment. I would argue that most of our patients are usually both expelling and communicating, and it is important for the analyst to be careful and attentive to find a way to contain and interpret the exact nature of the patient's internal conflicts and shape those interpretations to the degree of expelling or communicating that is being offered.

Some patients, particularly more disturbed narcissistic or borderline patients, will project themselves into the analyst and believe they possess the analyst's mind. So, these patients feel they are in fusion with the analyst and as a result see the analyst as a source of idealized knowledge, advice, or answers that belong to them. This patient is upset if they feel their property is being withheld, disrupted, or modified. Two other forms of projective identification identified by Rosenfeld have to do with the patient literally feeling they live within the analyst which provides the ultimate victory but also can become the worst inescapable trap.

Also, some patients phantasize they have become a parasite and are able to exist by simply possessing and feeding on the analyst, so they need not live their own lives anymore. While these last two situations are usually found in psychotic patients, the elements of these dynamics are also common with as-if patients who create identities based on what each person seems to want, need, or possess. With Joe, he seemed to try and adapt to what his wife wanted or what he imagined she needed, as well as what I and his girlfriend wanted and how I expected him to be in action and responsibility. But, in his efforts to clone our desires and shape himself into what we wished, he completely lost himself and felt empty, resentful, and envious. This left him with a frustrating behind-the-scenes strategy of revenge, manipulation, and control that gave him only temporary victories and very little in the way of true self-to-object intimacy and interaction.

As the paranoid or depressive patient draws closer to recognizing his destructive and controlling nature, he comes to face the pain, guilt, shame, and anxiety that come out of his love and concern for the object. When these phantasies of loss, revenge, and suffering were too unbearable and forgiveness seemed unreachable, narcissistic organizations and pathological bargains between self and object are seen as a last resort leading to more reliance on primitive mechanisms and intense use of projective identification.

CASE MATERIAL

In contrast to the thin-skinned (Rosenfeld 1987) nature of Joe with his confusing blend of paranoid and depressive conflicts and narcissistic transference, I will now illustrate some of the problems with the more destructive narcissist who operates within mostly a paranoid-schizoid realm with only a very primitive or immature foothold in the depressive position. Bill came to see me after his medical doctor suggested he talk to someone about his reactions to several life events.

Bill had always been the highest achiever in his classes and graduated college with several degrees in law and science. He told me he barely studied and "just knew the answers to most everything." Similarly, he reported he had always been a star athlete and "easily came in number one in most every sport he ever tried." All this was said in a somewhat arrogant and condescending tone. At the same time, Bill struck me as indeed being a very athletic man who was very smart.

Coming out of college, Bill was welcomed into a high-paying job in an important corporation. He worked there for several years but "always had the goal of starting up his own series of companies, selling them for a huge profit, making lots of money, and retiring early or just managing my portfolio." This was all said in a way that again made me feel judgmental, ready to put him in his place.

I noted this and added it to my internal list of transference/countertransference impressions with Joe that alternatively left me moved or unmoved, curious, reactive and defensive, or pushed to fix and cure. I tag such moments with a silent question mark, a sort of wait and see, study and watch for more information stance.

Bill quit his job to join a start-up financial venture in which he and the company were positioned to make a great deal of money and grow quickly. However, Bill told me he was "young and naive and never signed a contract and ended up screwed over by the partners and was left without any ownership in the company." So, Bill quit the job and went traveling to Europe with his earnings. He planned to "take it easy and spend sometime deciding what his next move would be." He told me this in a way that inflated himself and put down his job disaster as insignificant and inferior.

On his overseas trip, Bill had a skiing accident in which he was badly injured after his equipment malfunctioned. He was hospitalized for months and then had to engage in extensive rehabilitation. It was about a full year until he was able to pick up his life and start again. Indeed, there are some medical issues that may plague him at a later time. Bill found it difficult to find work since he had been out of circulation for a year. Then, he found a job which he thought was perfect, in which he would make lots of money and rise to power very quickly. After six months he bought a house and felt he was back in the game. However, a few months later the head of the company made some decisions that shifted the way the company operated, and this made Bill more of an ordinary worker bee instead of a standout director. He was still making a great deal of money and was quite important to the overall functioning of the corporation, but Bill felt he had been betrayed and demoted. He was angry and frustrated and tried to facilitate a change back to how things were originally but to no avail.

After about two years at the company, he decided he "wasn't going to stick around after they had lied to me and not provided me with the necessary tools to do my job." But, when he didn't receive an immediate abundance of interviews and when the few he did get turned him down, he was depressed and angry. He blamed the headhunters, the interviewers, the companies, and his analyst for not supporting him, helping him, and giving him what he needed and deserved. His destructive envy kicked in, and others were devalued.

So, many of Bill's sessions were filled with his anger and disappointment around not finding the job he imagined he should have. He said he had "lost some of the golden years, the time to pour the foundation of wealth and position." When I tried to engage him regarding his sense of personal failure and that he had missed the boat because of his injury and his misfortune, he usually reacted with spite and denial. I realized I was too quick in making these interpretations and was essentially taking his evacuative projections and returning these unwanted aspects of self to him without permission. He told me, "Maybe I will just stop this bullshit job search and go back to school and get another degree, and then no one will turn me down. I will be a necessity to them." I was struck by the combination of arrogance and desperation in his message. In these moments, he would sink into a period of self-loathing, but when I interpreted that, he seemed to feel like he was caught in the headlights and quickly blamed the economy, the region, the person who interviewed him, the "shitty medication the psychiatrist had put him on," or anything and anyone else who seemed handy. Or, Bill simply dismissed the whole thing as "meaningless and unimportant" and focused on how he would "call the shots and name his salary" after he came out of school again.

Of course, I was to blame as well. He attacked me in several ways. He told me, "This is completely useless. I get nothing out of this." Here, he was showing me that he devalued and attacked his objects so much with envy and malice that he was left with empty, useless objects. This strategy left him safe and victorious but alone and without any resources. I interpreted, "Is that because I am not giving you an instant cure, taking away all your problems right away? If I don't make it all better now, I am failing you?" Bill replied, "I don't see the point of this. I still feel crappy." I interpreted, "I think you see me as a magic pill that you take and feel better. But, you are starting to realize that instead you have to work with me to learn about what is going on inside of you and then we can find ways of changing things. But, I think this realization makes you angry."

This confrontation and interpretation seemed to lessen his anger and anxiety for a bit. Then, I added, "I think you are very angry and disappointed with yourself too." He said, "I was on track for so much. Now, I have wasted some of the best years of my life." Here, he was momentarily in touch with his narcissistic failure and sense of shame. He still saw himself as a star on the quick path to stardom, but he was admitting his shame and anger at being slowed down on that phantasy path.

When Bill simply sat there, looking at the floor, ignoring whatever I said and looking silent and sullen, he was viewing me as a dump site for his failure and I was supposed to recycle it into some type of better, happier product for him. He sat back while I was to do the dirty work.

During one session, he was telling me how he thought I was "doing absolutely nothing to help him and he felt exactly the same way as he did yesterday, so he didn't see the point of continuing." He spent most of the session in his usual stance of defiant anger, looking only at the ground and ignoring much of what I said. His responses were often merely a yes or no, much like an irritated adolescent. At the same time, Bill was clearly depressed and miserable, feeling and looking like a complete failure. However, most of the time, he blamed everyone else. Only on rare occasions would he include some comments about his fury with himself and how he "had wasted some of the prime years of his career." He never mentioned the lack of a relationship in his life unless I brought it up, and then he would agree that it was another area of failure, as if he was simply remembering another category of bitterness on a list of hated situations.

Because he was so much into attacking me and others for not providing him with what he felt he deserved, I interpreted that I must be really failing him, not giving him the immediate fix or answer he wants. I asked him how and why he was so frustrated with me. He replied in a loud and somewhat intimidating manner, "I could do better by smashing my fucking head against a wall. This therapy doesn't do anything for me. It is a complete waste of my time!" I replied, "Maybe we can try to find out how come you look to me and others to deliver everything but then we all seem to fail so much. It looks like you try and depend on someone and then you feel let down." He said, "That is not it at all! I don't know what you are talking about. I just want to get a better job and make more money at a position I enjoy with people I respect. I am sick of everything always getting in the way." I asked about what sort of things were not going his way. He told me, "For one thing, I can't stop thinking about my house and how to get rid of it now that it has no value to me." Of course, I was thinking that in the transference I was the house.

Bill explained that he had decided to default on his home payments since his house had lost a great deal of value since he bought it. He thought it was a "crummy investment that made no sense to keep." He told me he would sell it as a short sale and if the bank found out that he indeed had the funds to make his payments, then he would tell them he would walk away from it, "forcing them to back down and give me what I want." At this point, in the countertransference, I felt he was a liar and a cheat, hiding his large sums of money and pleading poverty only to dump what he didn't want and, if challenged, he would intimidate the object into doing his bidding. I wanted to tell him he was a bad, arrogant, person and all his problems were his fault, not anyone else's. I noticed these strong countertransference feelings and did my best to contain them and understand them.

With more libidinal narcissists like Joe, confrontation and interpretation work well together and help to break through the envy, arrogance, and denial long enough to provide the patient with a chance to explore his conflicts from a new perspective. This brings them into more of a depressive realm which then in turn brings on feelings of guilt, loss, and anxiety that are often so unbearable that they shift back to more paranoid narcissistic defenses. But, slow progress can be made in this way. However, the more destructive narcissist like Bill is not helped with this strategy. Confrontations only serve as an invitation to combat, and the envious attacks are escalated. So, containment and gradual interpretation of the terrible disappointment with their objects is a better avenue into helping the destructive narcissist to slowly face their emptiness and fear of difference and change.

So, after I had interpreted Bill's disappointment with me and all his objects, he agreed with me and seemed to settle down a bit. This seemed like the time to interpret his struggles with himself. So, I was shifting from an analyst-centered interpretation (Steiner 1994) to a patient-centered interpretation (Steiner 1994), something Kleinians have noticed to be important with this type of hard-to-reach patient. I interpreted, "You seemed pretty disappointed or fed up with yourself too." He replied, "'Fed up' pretty much sums it up. Yes, I am pissed at everyone, but mostly I am upset with myself that I have not met my expectations yet." Here, Bill was able to shift a bit from purely envious, destructive narcissism to a more depressive sense of failure. However, he was quick to try and restore his former state of psychic equilibrium (Joseph 1989) when he added, "It is only a matter of time before I bring to bear a package that will matter. On the job interviews, I am dealing with incompetents. If I could just get past those morons, I could show the people that really matter that I am the only one they would ever need." So, here he moved back to the place of seeing others as obstacles to his greatness rather than having to look at his own faults and limitations.

I have found that my more confrontational approach with thin-skinned narcissists such as my first patient Joe does not leave them feeling permanently hurt or damaged but actually helps them to think, at least momentarily, outside of their rigid, confining, and omnipotent stance regarding themselves as well as their objects. Interpreting how their destructiveness towards their objects and towards themselves is usually connected seems to have the best results rather than one or the other interpreted in isolation. Of course, the patient's level of responsiveness does have to do with if they are primarily libidinal or destructive in orientation and if their primary level of projective identification is communicative or evacuative and controlling.

With the more destructive narcissist, such as Bill, there is not much of a foothold in the depressive position so that any confrontations or even interpretations are almost immediately taken as an attack or put-down and are experienced as controlling or cruel. Even ongoing silent containment is difficult for the analyst because this more primitive type of patient tends to see most everything as a disappointment, a betrayal, or an entitlement and through projective identification pushes the analyst to act out, attack back, or retreat altogether.

The Kleinian school brings a remarkable clarity, hope, and technical wisdom to helping all patients find a way to trust, tolerate, change, love, and grow. Rosenfeld helped the patient understand that they were being understood. That was often the first time they had this experience, and it provided the first step towards building a new way to see themselves and others. The modern Kleinian approach and my own concept of analytic contact (Waska 2007) combines this clinical stance with other technical postures to create the greatest possible path to help the patient find their internal self, learn about the conflicts that cripple them, and gradually find the courage and knowledge to change. Transformation and choice begin to fill in what was so desolate, barren, and chaotic.

Conclusion

The modern Kleinian clinician uses the techniques originally discovered and described by Melanie Klein to help patients find respite and resolution from their internal torment. These clinical techniques have been expanded and extended by the contemporary followers of Klein and her insightful findings. In particular, the concept of Analytic Contact strongly endorses the regular interpretation of transference, projective identification, and phantasy as the cornerstone to healing. Close clinical attention is paid to the total transference and the complete countertransference as two important areas for information about the patient's immediate anxieties and phantasies and the best approach for containment and interpretation of these unconscious issues.

This book has described how today's practitioner typically treats a number of very disturbed and hard-to-reach patients who, while prone to intense acting out and early termination, are in great need of in-depth psychological reorganization. Regardless of diagnosis, length of treatment, or frequency of sessions, the technical approach of Analytic Contact and its focus on the utility of modern Kleinian procedures creates a clinical climate that offers patients a rich working-through process regardless of their internal difficulties. Many cases barely get off the ground due to levels of pathological conflict and destructive phantasy that make self/object connection extremely fragile. However, the modern Kleinian approach makes it possible to establish analytic contact with even the most chaotic situations and create a therapeutic experience that can be significant and meaningful. In doing so, there can be a healing process and the birth of new object relational experiences and interpersonal exchanges.

Where once the emotional river ran dry or stagnant, the water may flow again. Where once the banks overflowed and flooded, the waters can recede and flow in balance and with boundaries. Hope can be restored or perhaps established for the first time.

Bibliography

Akhtar, S. (1996). "Someday . . ." and "If Only . . ." Fantasies: Pathological Optimism and Inordinate Nostalgia as Related Forms of Idealization. *Journal of the American Psychoanalytic Association* 44: 723–753.

Anderson, M. (1999). The Pressure toward Enactment and the Hatred of Reality. *Journal of the American Psychoanalytic Association* 47(2): 503–518.

Bell, D. (1992). Hysteria: A Contemporary Kleinian Perspective. *British Journal of Psychotherapy* 9(2): 169–180.

Bianchedi, E. (1988). Theories on Anxiety in Freud and Melanie Klein: Their Metapsychological Status. *International Journal of Psychoanalysis* 69: 359–368.

Bicudo, V. (1964). Persecutory Guilt and Ego Restrictions: Characterization of a Pre-Depressive Position. *International Journal of Psychoanalysis* 45: 358–363.

Bion, W. (1959). Attacks on Linking. *International Journal of Psychoanalysis* 40: 308–315.

———. (1962a). *Learning from Experience.* London: Karnac.

———. (1962b). The Psycho-Analytic Study of Thinking. *International Journal of Psychoanalysis* 43: 306–310.

———. (1963). *Elements of Psychoanalysis.* New York: Basic Books.

Brenman, E. (1982). Separation: A Clinical Problem. *International Journal of Psycho-analysis* 63: 303–310.

Britton, R. (1998). *Belief and Imagination.* London: Routledge.

Cangnan, L. (2004). Contrasting Clinical Techniques: A British Kleinian, Contemporary Freudian and Latin American Kleinian Discuss Clinical Material. *International Journal of Psychoanalysis* 85(5): 1257–1260.

Engelbrecht, H. (1997). Report of the Ad Hoc Committee on the Crisis of Psychoanalysis: Challenges and Perspectives. *IPA Newsletter* 6: 53–59.

Espasa, F. (2002). Considerations on Depressive Conflict and Its Different Levels of Intensity: Implications for Technique. *International Journal of Psychoanalysis* 83(4): 825–836.

Feldman, M. (1992). The Manifestation of the Object in the Transference. *European Psychoanalytic Bulletin* 39: 69

———. (1994). Projective Identification in Phantasy and Enactment. *Psychoanalytic Inquiry* 14(2): 423–440.

———. (2004). Supporting Psychic Change: Betty Joseph. Pp. 20–35 in *In Pursuit of Psychic Change: The Betty Joseph Workshop,* edited by Hargreaves and Varchevker. London: Brunner-Routledge.

Grinberg, L. (1964). Two Kinds of Guilt: Their Relations with Normal and Pathological Aspects of Mourning. *International Journal of Psychoanalysis* 45: 366–371.

Grotstein, J. (1977). The Psychoanalytic Concept of Schizophrenia: I. The Dilemma. *International Journal of Psychoanalysis* 58: 403–425.

———. (1980a). The Significance of Kleinian Contributions to Psychoanalysis: Kleinian Instinct Theory Part One. *International Journal of Psychoanalytic Psychotherapy.* London: Jason Aronson, 375–392.

———. (1980b). The Significance of Kleinian Contributions to Psychoanalysis: Kleinian Instinct Theory Part Two. *International Journal of Psychoanalytic Psychotherapy.* London: Jason Aronson, 393–428.

———. (1982). Newer Perspectives in Object Relations Theory. *Contemporary Psychoanalysis* 18: 43–91.

———. (1985). A Proposed Revision of the Psychoanalytic Concept of the Death Instinct. *Yearbook of Psychoanalysis and Psychotherapy* 1: 299–326.

———. (2000). Some Considerations of "Hate" and a Reconsideration of the Death Instinct. *Psychoanalytic Inquiry* 20(2): 462–480.

————. (2005). The Voice from the Crypt. Paper presented for the Seventeenth Annual Melanie Klein Memorial Lectureship, sponsored by the Psychoanalytic Center of California, Los Angeles, Calif.

Hargreaves, E., and A. Varchevker. (2004). *In Pursuit of Psychic Change: The Betty Joseph Workshop*. London: Brunner-Routledge.

Heimann, P. (1956). Dynamics of Transference Interpretations. *International Journal of Psychoanalysis* 37: 303–310.

Isaacs, S. (1948). The Nature and Function of Phantasy. *International Journal of Psychoanalysis* 29: 73–97.

Joseph, B. (1983). On Understanding and Not Understanding: Some Technical Issues. *International Journal of Psychoanalysis* 64: 291–298.

————. (1985). Transference: The Total Situation. *International Journal of Psychoanalysis* 66: 447–454.

————. (1989). *Psychic Equilibrium and Psychic Change: Selected Papers of Betty Joseph*. The New Library of Psychoanalysis, vol. 9. London: Tavistock/Routledge.

————. (2000). Agreeableness as Obstacle. *International Journal of Psychoanalysis* 81(4): 641–649.

Kernberg, O. (2009). The Concept of the Death Instinct: A Clinical Perspective. *International Journal of Psychoanalysis* 90(5): 1009–1023.

Klein, M. (1928). Early Stages of the Oedipus Conflict. *International Journal of Psychoanalysis* 9: 167–180.

————. (1935). A Contribution to the Psychogenesis of Manic-Depressive States. *The Writings of Melanie Klein*, vol. 3. New York: Free Press.

————. (1940). Mourning and Its Relation to Manic-Depressive States. *International Journal of Psychoanalysis* 21: 125–153.

————. (1946). Notes on Some Schizoid Mechanisms. *The Writings of Melanie Klein*, vol. 3. Hogarth Press, 1–24.

————. (1952). The Origins of Transference. *International Journal of Psychoanalysis* 33: 433–438.

————. (1957). Envy and Gratitude. *The Writings of Melanie Klein*, vol. 3, Envy and Gratitude and Other Works. London: Hogarth Press, 1975, 176–235.

————. (1975). *Envy and Gratitude and Other Works 1946–1963*. Edited by M. Masud and R. Khan. The International Psychoanalytical Library, vol. 104.

Little, M. (1966). Transference in Borderline States. *International Journal of Psycho-analysis* 47: 476–485.

Malcolm, R. (1995). The Three W's: What, Where And When: The Rationale Of Interpretation. *International Journal of Psychoanalysis* 76: 447–456.

O'Shaughnessy, E. (1983). Words and Working Through. *International Journal of Psychoanalysis.* 64: 281–289.

Pick, I. (1985). Working Through in the Countertransference. *International Journal of Psychoanalysis* 66: 157–166.

Potamianou, A. (1992). *Un Bouclier dans L'Economie des Etats Limites L'Espoir.* Paris: Presses University, France.

Quinodoz, J. (1993). *The Taming of Solitude: Separation Anxiety in Psychoanalysis.* New York: Routledge.

———. (1996). The Sense of Solitude in the Psychoanalytic Encounter. *International Journal of Psychoanalysis* 77: 481–496.

Rey, J. (1988). That Which Patients Bring to Analysis. *International Journal of Psychoanalysis* 69: 457–470.

Rosenfeld, H. (1971). Contributions to the Psychopathology of Psychotic Patients: The Importance of Projective Identification in the Ego Structure and Object Relations of the Psychotic Patient. In *Problems of Psychosis,* edited by P. Daucet and C. McLaurin. Amsterdam: Excerpta Medica.

———. (1974). A Discussion of the Paper by Ralph R. Greenson on "Transference: Freud or Klein." *International Journal of Psychoanalysis* 55: 49–51.

———. (1983). Primitive Object Relations and Mechanisms. *International Journal of Psychoanalysis* 64: 261.

———. (1987). Afterthought: Changing Theories and Changing Techniques in Psychoanalysis. Pp. 265–279 in *Impasse and Interpretation.* London: Tavistock.

———. (1988). Contributions to the Psychopathology of Psychotic Patients: The Importance of Projective Identification and the Ego Structure and Object Relations of the Psychotic Patient. In *Melanie Klein Today: Developments in Theory and Practice,* vol. 1, Mainly Theory, edited by Elizabeth Bott Spillius. London: Routledge.

Roth, P. (2001). Mapping the Landscape: Levels of Transference Interpretation. *International Journal of Psychoanalysis* 82(3): 533–543.

Schafer, R. (1994a). The Contemporary Kleinians of London. *Psychoanalytic Quarterly* 63: 409–432.

———. (1994b). Commentary: Traditional Freudian and Kleinian Freudian Analysis. *Psychoanalytic Inquiry* 14(3): 462–475.

———. (1997). Current Trends in Psychoanalysis in the USA. Essays, in *IPA Newsletter* 6: 1.

Schoenhals, H. (1996). Triangular Space and Symbolization. *Psychoanalytic Inquiry* 16: 167–183.

Searles, H. (1977). The Analyst's Participant Observation as Influenced by the Patient's Transference. *Contemporary Psychoanalysis* 13: 367–370.

Segal, H. (1972). A Delusional System as a Defense against Re-Emergence of a Catastrophic Situation. *International Journal of Psychoanalysis* 53: 393–403.

———. (1977). Psychoanalytic Dialogue: Kleinian Theory Today. *Journal of the American Psychoanalytic Association* 25: 363.

———. (1983). Some Clinical Implications of Melanie Klein's Work: Emergence from Narcissism. *International Journal of Psychoanalysis* 64: 269–276.

———. (1993a). On the Clinical Usefulness of the Death Instinct. *International Journal of Psychoanalysis* 74: 55–61.

———. (1993b). An Interview with Hanna Segal: By Virginia Hunter. *Psychoanalytic Review* 80: 1–28.

Sodre, I. (2004). Discussion of Feldman's Chapter. P. 36 in *In Pursuit of Psychic Change: The Betty Joseph Workshop*, edited by Hargreaves and Varchevker. London: Brunner-Routledge.

Spillius, E. (1996). Paper presented at A Day with Elizabeth Bott Spillius, San Francisco Psychoanalytic Institute, San Francisco, Calif.

———. (1983). Some Developments from the Work of Melanie Klein. *International Journal of Psychoanalysis* 64: 321–332.

———. (1993). Varieties of Envious Experience. *International Journal of Psychoanalysis* 74: 1199–1212.

Stein, R. (1990). A New Look at the Theory of Melanie Klein. *International Journal of Psychoanalysis* 71: 499–511.

Steiner, J. (1984). Some Reflections on the Analysis of Transference: A Kleinian View. *Psychoanalytic Inquiry* 4(3): 443–463.

——. (1987). The Interplay between Pathological Organizations and the Paranoid-Schizoid and Depressive Positions. *International Journal of Psychoanalysis* 68: 69–80.

——. (1989). The Psychoanalytic Contribution of Herbert Rosenfeld. *International Journal of Psychoanalysis* 70: 611–616.

——. (1990). Pathological Organizations as Obstacles to Mourning: The Role of Unbearable Guilt. *International Journal of Psychoanalysis* 71: 87–94.

——. (1992). The Equilibrium between the Paranoid-Schizoid and the Depressive Positions. Pp. 46–58 in *Clinical Lectures on Klein and Bion*, New Library of Psychoanalysis, vol. 14. London: Routledge.

——. (1993). *Psychic Retreats: Pathological Organizations in Psychotic, Neurotic and Borderline Patients*. New York: Routledge.

——. (1994). Patient-Centered and Analyst-Centered Interpretations: Some Implications of Containment and Countertransference. *Psychoanalytic Inquiry* 14(3): 406–422.

——. (1998). Transference and Its Impact on Education. International Psychoanalytic Association Inter-Regional Conferences, International Psychoanalytic Association Website, 2000.

——. (2000). Containment, Enactment, and Communication. *International Journal of Psychoanalysis*. 81: 245–255.

——. (2008). *Rosenfeld in Retrospect: Essays on His Clinical Influence*, edited by John Steiner. London: Routledge.

Strachey, J. (1934). The Nature of the Therapeutic Action of Psychoanalysis. *International Journal of Psychoanalysis* 15: 127–159.

Tyson, R. (1998). The International Psychoanalytical Association: Why, When, Where, and How. Home Pages. *IPA Newsletter* 7: 1.

Waska, R. (2002). *Primitive Experiences of Loss: Working with the Paranoid-Schizoid Patient*. London: Karnac.

——. (2005). *Real People, Real Problems, Real Solutions: The Kleinian Approach to Difficult Patients*. London: Brunner/Rutledge.

————. (2006). *The Danger of Change: The Kleinian Approach with Patients Who Experience Progress as Trauma.* London: Brunner/Rutledge.

————. (2007). *The Concept of Analytic Contact: A Kleinian Approach to Reaching the Hard to Reach Patient.* London: Brunner/Rutledge.

————. (2010a). *Treating Severe Depressive and Persecutory Anxieties States: Using Analytic Contact to Transform the Unbearable.* London: Karnac, in press.

————. (2010b). *Love, Hate, and Knowledge: The Kleinian Method of Analytic Contact and the Future of Psychoanalysis.* London: Karnac, in press.

————. (2010c). *Moments of Uncertainty in Psychoanalytic Practice: Interpreting within the Matrix of Projective Identification, Countertransference, and Enactment.* New York: Columbia University Press, in press.

————. (2010d). *Selected Theoretical and Clinical Issues in Psychoanalytic Psychotherapy: A Modern Kleinian Approach to Analytic Contact.* New York: Novoscience, in press.

Winnicott, D. W. (1974). Fear of Breakdown. Pp. 173–182 in *The British School of Psychoanalysis: The Independent Tradition,* ed. G. Kohon. London: Free Association Books, 1986.

Index

abuse: of containment, 40–41; of object, 40–41; by parents, 72, 73, 98, 112–14, 118–19

acting out, xi, xii; countertransference, 58, 83, 85, 86, 88, 89, 91, 95, 96, 98, 100, 110, 126, 133, 146; Feldman on, 22–23

age, 5, 6

alcoholism, 6, 51, 73, 118

ambition, 141

analyst: acceptance of, 73; acting out by, 58, 83, 85, 86, 88, 89, 91, 95, 96, 98, 100, 110, 126, 133, 146; anxiety of, 46; boundaries with, 36–38, 40–41, 140; complacency of, 10; confrontation by, 125–26, 129–31, 132, 134, 143; containment by, 22–23, 31, 40, 64, 78, 86, 109–10, 122, 135; control of, 88, 99; devaluing of, 11, 13–14, 44, 135, 143; disclosure to, 92–93; as dominant, 79, 84, 88, 89; Feldman on, 85; flirtation with, 9, 88–89, 92, 96; idealization, 64, 68,

79–80, 97–98, 99; independence of, 91–94, 101, 137; judgment by, 72, 88, 141, 144; as love object, 36, 40–41; as peer, 79–80, 89; as property, 140; rejection by, 88; rejection of, 86, 93–94, 95–96, 98, 137; as threat, 137; workload of, 105. *See also* countertransference

Analytic Contact, vii; creation of, 107–8; goal of, viii, 67, 108–9; here-and-now focus of, 51; loss with, 109; narcissism with, 135; phantasies with, 76–77; time in, 105, 106, 107, 108; transformation with, 67

anger: as control, 90, 91; of David (Chapter 1), 19; of Jack, 58; passivity with, 18, 19, 128, 132; of Sue (Chapter 5), 90; with transference, 55, 58, 60, 63, 68, 69, 72, 74, 75, 79, 88, 90, 91, 111–12; violence and, 121

anxiety: of analyst, 46; containment of, 111, 122; control as, 53–54, 60; covering up, 59–60, 68–69;

About the Author

Robert Waska, MFT, PhD, is a graduate of the Institute for Psychoanalytic Studies and has a private psychoanalytic practice for individuals and couples in San Francisco and Marin County. Dr. Waska has taught and presented in the Bay Area as well as internationally. He is the author of ten published textbooks on psychoanalytic theory and technique, is a contributing author for both *The Handbook of Contemporary Psychotherapy* and *The Handbook of Hate*, and has published over eighty articles in professional journals.

Dr. Waska's work focuses on various contemporary Kleinian topics including projective identification, loss, borderline and psychotic states, the practical realities of psychoanalytic practice in the modern world, and the establishment of analytic contact with difficult, hard-to-reach patients. He emphasizes the moment-to-moment understanding of transference and phantasy as the vehicle for gradual integration and mastery of unconscious conflict between self and other.

Breinigsville, PA USA
29 April 2010
237099BV00003B/7/P